SELF-LOVE WORKBOOK
FOR WOMEN

SELF-LOVE
WORKBOOK
FOR WOMEN

Release Self-Doubt, Build Self-Compassion, and Embrace Who You Are

MEGAN LOGAN, MSW, LCSW

ROCKRIDGE
PRESS

For general information on our other products and services or to obtain technical support, please contact our Customer Care Department within the United States at (866) 744-2665, or outside the United States at (510) 253-0500.

Rockridge Press publishes its books in a variety of electronic and print formats. Some content that appears in print may not be available in electronic books, and vice versa.

Interior and Cover Designer: Liz Cosgrove
Art Producer: Samantha Ulban
Editor: Emily Angell
Production Editor: Rachel Taenzler

Illustrations used under license from Shutterstock.com.

ISBN: Print 978-1-64739-729-6
eBook 978-1-64876-258-1
R0

This Workbook
Belongs To:

CONTENTS

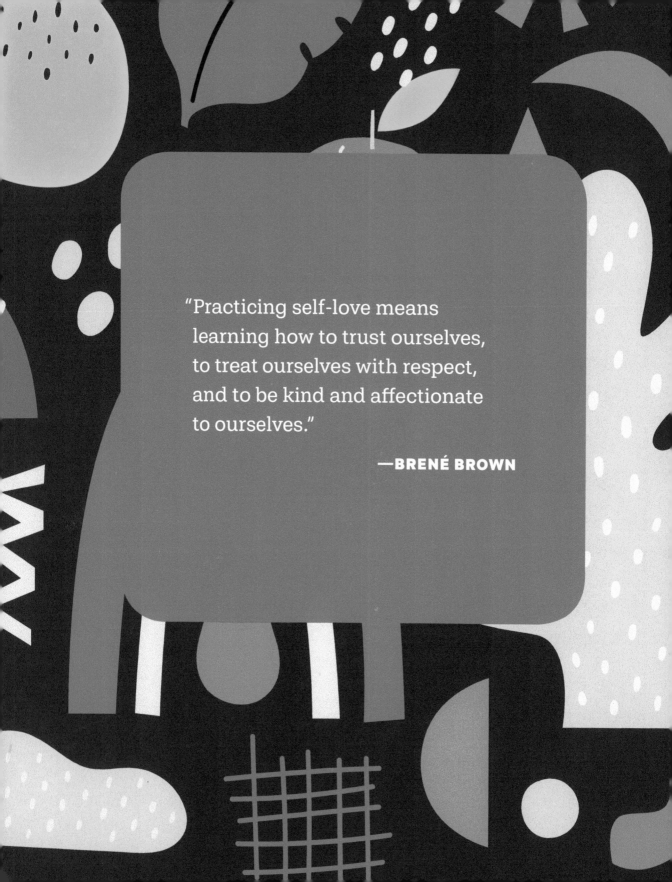

"Practicing self-love means learning how to trust ourselves, to treat ourselves with respect, and to be kind and affectionate to ourselves."

—BRENÉ BROWN

INTRODUCTION

WELCOME! As you embark on your journey toward self-love, I am excited to help you navigate by introducing you to a road map that will lead you toward a better relationship with yourself. I want to praise you for taking this big step forward. As women, we often struggle to set aside time for ourselves. This workbook is designed not just to talk about self-love and why it is important, but to show you how to find it.

Experts often talk about how important it is to have self-worth. Yet, how do we simply love ourselves? Wouldn't it be nice if it were as easy as just knowing the definition of self-love? I have found that the pathway to self-love must include intentional practice, with mindful focus and energy devoted toward developing those skills. If self-love is the destination, the activities in this book are the fueling stations along the way. Your willingness to complete and practice the exercises is the fuel that will get you there.

Sometimes this process may feel like it takes too much effort or just doesn't ring true. You may hit speed bumps or take a detour. It's okay, since just as with true self-love, we are not focused on outcomes but on the process itself. Keep practicing! You are worth it, and purchasing this workbook is a wonderful first step toward making yourself a priority. Eventually your hard work will pay off and you will be on your way to loving yourself.

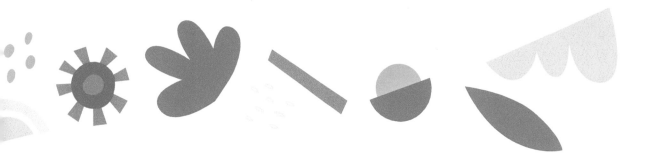

Through my personal experience, and in my 20 years as a licensed clinical social worker specializing in women's issues, I have witnessed firsthand the importance of self-love. As a working mother in a helping profession, I have found myself running out of gas at the end of the day, my battery drained. Depleted, I wanted to zone out with Netflix and chocolate. Avoiding social connections because they felt too draining caused some problems in my life, leading to isolation and feeling burned out. It was in these moments that I realized how important it was to put myself first. Today, I work to help my clients do the same—to turn within and learn how to prioritize self-care and love.

Something amazing happens when women learn to find and nurture their gifts and strengths and begin to heal their lives. Whether you're recovering from a distorted body image, leaving an unhealthy relationship, or simply deciding to put yourself first, this book provides helpful tools and exercises for creating a life filled with meaning and purpose. Through the use of affirmations and mantras, step-by-step practices, exercises, and thought-provoking prompts, this workbook encourages movement toward greater self-love. Having said that, please understand that this book is not meant to replace therapy, medication, or mental health treatment, and there is no shame in reaching out to a health-care provider for any help you may need. Rather, this workbook can serve as a wonderful adjunct for healing and growth. I like to think of it as a starting place and a map to show you the way.

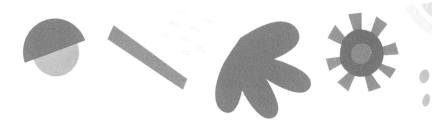

This book is broken into two parts. In part 1, you'll gain an understanding of self-love while recognizing why it's so important to make it a priority. Part 2 breaks the concept of self-love into separate components, including chapters on releasing self-doubt, practicing self-compassion, building your self-worth, and creating healthier relationships, as well as activities throughout to practice and encourage self-reflection and inspiration.

It is perfectly fine to move at your own pace; in fact, I encourage you to not rush the process. Remember that this is a journey, and it will lead to many destinations, including a place of wisdom from which you are able to practice kindness and compassion toward yourself.

I am hopeful that as you go through this workbook, the lessons will be paved with your courage and willingness to be vulnerable. Some of these introspective prompts and activities may feel scary or overwhelming at times. Please try to make space and allow these feelings to be present as you move forward and practice the skills. Don't worry if that sounds impossible—I will help support and encourage you along the way.

I am so excited to ride along as your copilot as you grow, learn, heal, and ultimately know what a gift you are in this world. Thank you for trusting me and allowing me to share in your experience.

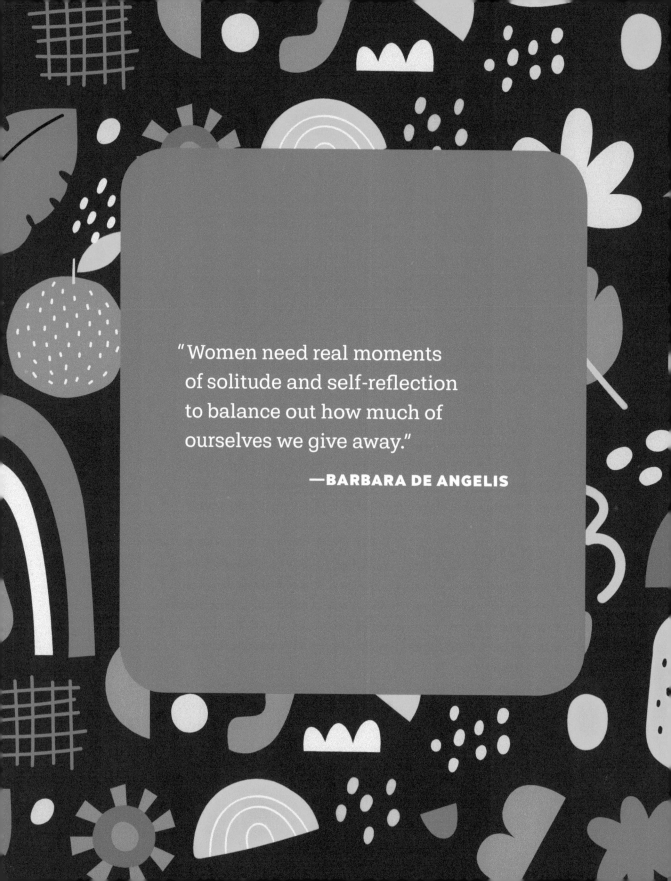

"Women need real moments of solitude and self-reflection to balance out how much of ourselves we give away."

—BARBARA DE ANGELIS

PART ONE

Let's Talk about Self-Love

Before beginning any journey, you must have an idea of where to begin and your final destination. The first leg of this journey involves laying a foundation for understanding self-love. This part of the workbook will allow you to take time to reflect and consider what self-love means to you and identify areas that you are already strong in and other areas that need growth. Part 1 provides the purpose for learning self-love. It also serves as the "why" for taking the time and making space to complete the exercises in part 2.

ONE
THE LOWDOWN ON SELF-LOVE

"And I would find myself again. Not the same version of me that I was looking for, but a stronger version. A wiser version. A woman who knew that she was enough, just as she was. A woman who had been tried in the fire but instead of being burned by it, came out gold. A woman who finally, after doubting and questioning and striving and hustling for her worth for years . . . finally, finally came to the realization that she was and is and has always been . . . *enough*."

—MANDY HALE

To start, we must first drill down into the idea of self-love in order to fuel up with motivation and energy. This chapter will help inspire and prepare you to do the work in part 2. Here, we'll come to better understand and conceptualize the nebulous idea of self-love by defining what it is, what it isn't, and what it might look like on a daily basis. There's an assessment exercise at the end of this chapter to help you get a quick snapshot of where you stand in the self-love arena.

WHAT IS SELF-LOVE?

Self-love is the fuel that allows an individual to reach their full potential, and is filled with compassion, grace, and gentleness. Making space and prioritizing ourselves allows us to embrace our lives completely and wholeheartedly. Self-love is learning to extend kindness toward ourselves, even when we struggle and suffer. It is extending forgiveness to ourselves when we make mistakes. Self-love means prioritizing ourselves and giving ourselves permission to find and believe in our strengths and gifts. Sometimes it means putting ourselves first. Sometimes it means making space to identify our needs and wants. It involves setting boundaries, and setting boundaries involves self-love. These two concepts work together.

The clients I work with often struggle to know how to love themselves. Often, in the first therapy session, women can quickly and easily identify some internalized shame-based beliefs and the need for self-love, but then they get stuck, not knowing what steps to take next in order to change. They become lost, unfamiliar with how to navigate the path forward.

WHAT IT ISN'T

To better understand what self-love involves, sometimes it helps to think about what self-love *doesn't* involve. Self-love is not perfection, nor is it always being happy. It is not based on your achievements and external measurements of success. It is not rooted in shame-based criticism or fear. It does not shame, lie, minimize, or criticize. Often, women think that they can love themselves through fault-finding and beating themselves up, as if this will help them become a better version of themselves. If you can relate, I can promise you that in the effort to make yourself better through self-shaming and self-criticism, you will become worse and broken-down, waiting for someone or something to rescue you. True self-love must come from within, even when we screw up or take a wrong turn in life.

WHY DO WE STRUGGLE TO LOVE OURSELVES?

Self-love seems like a simple enough concept. But why does it prove so elusive? All humans are hardwired for connection and belonging. For women, nurturing has its roots in survival. In early hunting and gathering societies, women's activities centered around bearing and rearing children, gathering food and drink, and creating a safe home space. Today, as women, we often find ourselves taking care of our children, our parents, our friends, our lovers. We extend grace and compassion toward others so easily, yet we often struggle to make space and time to put ourselves first. Perhaps this stems from a faulty belief that we are selfish or undeserving. Maybe it comes from internalized societal messages, early childhood wounds, or deeply rooted trauma. Or perhaps we just don't take the time to prioritize ourselves.

Internalized beliefs of unworthiness are rooted in shame, and where there is shame, self-love struggles to grow. I have found that most women struggling to love themselves have a strong, critical internal voice. Rarely would they speak to their friends, family, or even an enemy the way they talk to themselves. Over time, this internalized, critical narrative creates an automatic narrative; a well-worn pathway like an eight-lane superhighway. While learning to practice self-love can sometimes feel like using a butter knife to chop down weeds and make a path through the thick jungle, just know that creating a new narrative and doing the exercises in this workbook will soon make way for a clearer and healthier pathway to emerge.

Likewise, if you had a difficult childhood that was rooted in dysfunctional patterns, self-love may never have had a chance to take root and blossom. It is never too late to start that process. We can learn how to love ourselves even as adults and create new, solid foundations for growth and healing.

WHERE DOES A LACK OF SELF-LOVE SHOW UP FOR YOU?

A woman who sacrifices her own needs and desires for everyone else is likely to eventually become resentful and frustrated. At first, it might look like giving and nurturing. Over time, she loses her sense of self and becomes exhausted, bitter, and unfulfilled.

The reasons behind a lack of self-love are plenty, and the manifestations of an empty self-love tank may show up in many ways. The reasons might include hating our bodies, and the manifestations might be engaging in destructive patterns like dieting, binging and purging, compulsively body checking, and comparing ourselves to others on social media. It might look like getting caught in an endless chase for emotionally unavailable or inappropriate partners in the fruitless attempt to feel special or wanted. It might look like staying in unhealthy relationships much longer than needed. A lack of self-love reveals itself when we focus on finding external sources to fuel us. This often leaves us feeling even emptier inside.

Less obviously, sometimes a lack of self-love shows up disguised as perfectionism. This may sound strange at first. Wouldn't accomplishments and success foster self-love? Unfortunately, when perfectionism and external measurements of self-worth take the wheel, self-love comes to a screeching halt. Instead, feelings of unworthiness take over and move us in the wrong direction, away from self-love. Have you ever thought, *If only I get 100 percent on my math test. If only I lose 20 pounds. If only I had a romantic partner.*

Hustling to prove to others and ourselves that we are worthy becomes an endless, empty pursuit that mistakenly feels like self-love. It is not. Self-love is what shines through even when we *don't* accomplish our goals or meet our measurements of success. Self-love must involve extending kindness and grace to ourselves, no matter the outcome. Later in this workbook, you'll have an opportunity to put this idea into practice.

THE BENEFITS OF LOVING YOURSELF

Imagine for a moment what your life would look like if you truly loved yourself. What would change if you let go of self-doubt, self-criticism, and the fear of not being good enough? Imagine a life where you feel whole, energized, and ready to take on whatever life hands you. Imagine feeling that you are worthy and have meaning in this world. You have just identified the benefits of loving yourself.

Here are five ways loving yourself can change your life:

1. **A kinder, gentler you.** Imagine talking to yourself in a loving and supportive way. Kind of like a best friend, coach, parent, or teacher. Being supportive, encouraging, and forgiving allows for grace and peace to come into your life.

2. **More energy for living fully.** Freeing up space and time to nurture yourself and practice self-care allows for a renewal of energy and an endless supply of fuel that comes from within. It's like a well that never runs out of water.

3. **More love to share with others.** Cliché, but so true! It's hard to love someone else the way you want to if you don't first love yourself, and you may fall into a pattern of dependency or need. Loving yourself more will have a positive impact on all of your relationships.

4. **Healthier relationships with loved ones.** Without self-love to fuel our own lives, we will feel the need to look elsewhere, and sometimes that takes the form of attempting to find fuel in relationships with others. Unfortunately, these relationships can become imbalanced and filled with need, resentment, and bitterness, as we look to others to make us happy or help us feel worthy. Learning to self-love allows us to have healthier dynamics and expectations in relationships. *We* become the creators of our happiness.

5. **No longer dependent on external measures of success.** Of course, it feels wonderful to be successful and reach your goals. When self-love fuels this rather than self-doubt and fear, success becomes something to enjoy and appreciate with gratitude and a strong sense of our gifts.

WHY WOMEN SHOULD MAKE SELF-LOVE A PRIORITY

Self-love is an essential nutrient in our lives. We can nourish ourselves fully by practicing self-care and self-compassion. Self-love, rooted in knowing and nurturing internal strengths and grounded in personal values, is essential for growth, learning, and the fullness that comes with living your whole truth. Stretching outward, the sentiment "you can't pour from an empty cup" illustrates how our own inner stores affect our ability to be anything to anybody. Rarely, if ever, does true love extend beyond ourselves if there is no source from within. Running around trying to be worthy and please everyone is exhausting and ultimately leaves us feeling depleted. Self-critical messages, while falsely seeming to motivate, prove counterproductive, driving a sense of disconnection, resentment, and loneliness. Without self-love, opportunities set in for unhealthy tendencies, such as self-destructive relationship patterns, codependency, people-pleasing, addictions, and self-sabotage. When we don't prioritize self-love, we hustle to be "good enough" by measuring outcomes like the number on the scale, a grade on a test, how many friends we have. These measurements fall short of true self-love that comes from within. Prioritizing and practicing self-love is imperative to allowing ourselves to find peace, have meaningful relationships and connections, and reach our fullest potential. Imagine the amazing things that can happen with that kind of self-love.

Before starting any journey, you'll want to identify what you hope to get out of the experience. It can help to slow down, quiet the chatter in your mind, and relax your body to allow your inner wisdom to speak to you. Find a quiet place to sit, read through the following instructions, and then practice the steps below:

1. Start by gently closing your eyes.

2. Take three deep breaths, inhaling fully and exhaling slowly.

3. Think back to what prompted you to buy this workbook. Pay attention to any silent nudges or places that might feel uncomfortable. Reflect for a moment on what you hope to gain from this workbook. Think about how you might feel in your body if you were to fully love yourself. Pay attention to the changes in your body and your breathing.

4. Relax and open your eyes when you're ready.

HOW TO START YOUR SELF-LOVE JOURNEY

Ready, set, let's go! To get started, let's first take a look at how to prepare to begin our journey. Here are a few things you will need:

- **Time.** You'll want to find time with minimal distractions. In the real world, women often find themselves in many roles, and that means multitasking. As a working mother, I vividly recall once breast-feeding my child while wearing a baby sling, stirring spaghetti sauce, and being on a work conference call. Not ideal for deep reflection and introspection! When doing this workbook, try setting aside even 15 minutes of alone and quiet time. It could mean waking up 15 minutes earlier or going to bed 15 minutes later. You might even want to sneak the workbook into the bathroom!

- **Colored pens or pencils; craft materials.** In addition to this workbook, I encourage you to find some special colored pens or pencils. Sometimes using a specific pen or special, colored writing utensils can bring the journaling experience to life. Colors, textures, and different styles of writing remind us to prioritize ourselves, and tend to make the experience more enjoyable.

- **A special place.** When you begin this process, it's important to find the right space to ensure comfort and a relaxed state of mind. Perhaps a comfy chair with some pillows and a blanket will do, or a special place in your home where it is quiet and calm. I have one client who uses her closet to find privacy.

- **A ritual and sensory experience.** To enhance the experience, try lighting a candle, playing some spa relaxation music, adding soft lighting, cuddling up in pajamas, and drinking some hot tea. The idea is to create a ritual and intentional practice filled with multisensory experiences. Such a soothing and nurturing atmosphere opens you up to the possibilities of self-love.

- **An open mind and willingness to be vulnerable.** Perhaps the most important tool when starting your journey is the willingness to welcome vulnerability. When you're honest and authentic with yourself, creativity, growth, and healing can flourish. Open yourself up to the possibilities, and when feeling scared or overwhelmed, just notice and acknowledge the feelings, take a deep breath, and shift your focus back to the workbook.

CHALLENGES YOU MAY FACE ALONG THE WAY

When working on topics like self-love, you may find yourself on a bumpy road at times, hitting potholes or even breaking down on the side of the road. These challenges may come in the form of self-doubt, fear, being too busy, distractions, a fear of being too self-indulgent, or feelings of not being worthy enough to even get started. Please be patient with yourself and know that you are worth it. Don't give up! Keep moving forward, even (and maybe especially) when facing these obstacles. Even if you take the time and read a chapter but can't do the exercises, it's okay. If there is a chapter or section of the workbook that just seems too hard or doesn't resonate with you, feel free to come back to it when the time is right, or skip to a section that fits your needs at that moment. This is your journey and, at the very least, you'll want to practice kindness and self-compassion while using this book. The exercises in this workbook can be used on their own, in partnership with a therapist, or even with a small group of women to support and encourage each other.

IT WON'T HAPPEN OVERNIGHT

Healing rarely happens quickly. In fact, true change takes time. You might feel like you are stuck on a merry-go-round, but sometimes growth is nonlinear—it can have ups and downs. Please try to trust the process and journey. Be gentle and kind to yourself when you feel impatient and struggle to feel self-love. Like a caterpillar and a seed must progress through stages to soar and bloom, you are evolving and growing, and this is a journey of miles rather than minutes. Allow yourself to learn each step of the way.

HOW SELF-LOVE CAN CHANGE YOUR LIFE

Truly loving yourself can transform your life on so many levels. Imagine, just for a moment, what life would feel like if fueled from the inside, rather than by external measurements of success based on societal standards or others' expectations. The energy that can come from self-love will propel you into becoming the best version of yourself. No longer trapped in the pursuit of hopeless relationships, emotionally unavailable partners, people-pleasing, self-doubt, jealousy, envy, or destructive behaviors. When self-worth grows from within, love blossoms and spreads to the outside world, making relationships more enriched and authentic. With self-love, you become free to make mistakes and still move about in the world, all the time learning and growing.

Self-Assessment: Where Are You in Your Self-Love Journey?

Let's see where you are in your journey toward self-love. Rate these statements on a scale of 0 to 5, and when finished, add up the total score.

0 = never   1 = rarely   2 = sometimes   3 = frequently   4 = most often   5 = always

1. **I believe I am worthy and deserving of love.**

   0   1   2   3   4   5

2. **I believe I am special.**

   0   1   2   3   4   5

3. **I believe I have a purpose for living.**

   0   1   2   3   4   5

4. **I am able to communicate my needs and wants.**

   0   1   2   3   4   5

5. **I am accepting and loving of my body just the way it looks.**

   0   1   2   3   4   5

6. **I do not need to be in a romantic relationship to feel whole.**

   0   1   2   3   4   5

7. I think it is okay to make mistakes and not be the best.

0   1   2   3   4   5

8. My feelings matter as much as everyone else's.

0   1   2   3   4   5

9. I place equal importance on my feelings as on other people's feelings.

0   1   2   3   4   5

10. I deserve good things in my life.

0   1   2   3   4   5

Scoring:

40–50 = You have achieved a wonderful sense of self-love. Keep growing and loving yourself.

30–40 = You're on your way. Keep taking time to remember you are special and important.

20–30 = There are times you feel worthy and other times you struggle. Keep working and believing in yourself.

10–20 = You struggle to feel worthy and loved. You are in the right place to learn how to love yourself.

0–10 = It's time to build a new foundation for you to develop self-love. Keep reading—you deserve it.

CONCLUSION

I am so proud of you for your willingness and courage to take the first step of our journey together. Your recognition of the importance of self-love will hopefully sustain you through the next chapter as we prepare ourselves to delve further into the practice of self-love. You have taken the first and most important step, which is acknowledging the importance of self-love in your life. Let's keep moving forward to the next leg of our journey.

I've included an affirmation at the end of each chapter. An affirmation is a great tool for relaxing and focusing the mind, encouraging positive thinking, and affirming who you are and who you can become. Take a moment to focus on your breath and repeat this statement to yourself until you are ready to turn the page.

Opening myself up to vulnerability is where the magic happens.

TWO

PREPARE FOR THE ROAD AHEAD

"If someone else notices our qualities and talents, we think those parts of us must be worthwhile. . . . We long for someone to discover us, admire us, colonize us. But why must it be another person? Why can't *you* sail that voyage and explore yourself?"

—VIRONIKA TUGALEVA

The next step in the self-love journey involves preparation. In this chapter, we'll take steps to establish a purposeful process and create a space for intentional practice in learning to love ourselves. You will explore ways to become vulnerable and authentic, and learn how to make yourself a priority in a world in which other things compete for your attention. Think of this chapter as making sure you have your proverbial full tank of gas, inflated tires, a working engine, seatbelts, airbags, and jumper cables handy. (And remember that sometimes music and snacks to enjoy during the ride can enhance the experience.) While finding self-love can feel magical in itself, this happens best in the context of dedication and commitment. So buckle up—you're worth it.

THE POWER OF A DAILY
SELF-LOVE PRACTICE

Each day presents itself as a new opportunity to reset and reawaken self-love. If you struggled the day before to set aside time and make yourself a priority, it's okay. It is never too late to start practicing self-love. Through it all, try talking to yourself in a kind and support-ive way so you will stay focused on your goals. Self-love can't grow in the context of shame and put-downs. Imagine if you spoke kindly and lovingly to yourself every day. What would change? What would feel different? What would you give yourself permission to do?

A daily self-love practice sets up a pathway in the brain for self-love to become automatic, just like brushing your teeth. Scientists have learned that activated neurons connect to other firing neurons in the brain to transmit information. These neurons wire together to create a neural pathway. With daily practice, any new action—in this case, self-love—becomes ingrained. Sure, in the beginning, this is challenging. It feels like work or maybe even self-indulgent at times. Nevertheless, if continued, this new behavior will become second nature, allowing for self-love to grow.

IT'S NOT ALL BUBBLE BATHS AND
MANICURES

I used to think that self-love sounded indulgent and luxurious. Who has time for that when work, families, and relationships demand so much of our energy and time? I quickly learned that living fully requires that we nurture ourselves well beyond the scope of getting a manicure, drinking a glass of wine, and soaking in the tub. Sure, relaxation and pampering are lovely and essential. But true self-love involves more. It means we develop honesty within ourselves, identify our values, and create an authentic life free from self-harm and self-destructive patterns. It's about creating a life in which our choices and decisions nurture and reflect our true selves and values. Consider this for a moment. What priorities would shift and change for you? Don't worry if you aren't clear about values yet. We'll explore that in the second part of our workbook. Just remember, while bubble baths and manicures are fun, true self-love comes from deep within and does not rely on external events, outcomes, other people's opinions, or societal standards.

BE VULNERABLE

As women, we often find ourselves in the nurturer role, taking care of and helping others. It is difficult to notice that we, too, may need to feel special or loved. Focusing on others' needs can be a way of avoiding our own needs, which can make us feel vulnerable. An important part of being authentic to ourselves is recognizing our vulnerabilities—our feelings of not being good enough, along with our disappointment, sadness, and fears—and making a conscious choice to "go there." Practicing honesty and vulnerability within ourselves can sometimes feel overwhelming and scary, but it's necessary for coming to terms with any obstacles to inner peace and self-acceptance. While you are your own number-one supporter in this journey, consider identifying trusted relationships for support; perhaps a friend, family member, partner, or therapist. These supportive people can help cheer you on and encourage you from the side of the road. Remember that you are in the driver's seat, and the ability to let yourself be vulnerable ultimately begins with you.

BE HONEST

If vulnerability is our friend, then honesty is her sister. Honesty happens when we cultivate authenticity. By living only to please others or meet external standards, we pull away from our true paths. Honesty allows for us to thoughtfully speak our minds and express our feelings and opinions, even if it upsets others or makes someone else uncomfortable. When we suppress our thoughts and feelings, they often come out in forms that cause grief and discomfort. Suppressing emotions does not make them go away. In reality, it can cause feelings to stay around longer and intensify. Over time, stifling negative emotions contributes to health-related issues such as high blood pressure, memory issues, and difficulty focusing. Unexpressed and unresolved anger can build, leading to an overreaction that can damage relationships and self-worth.

Being true to ourselves involves recognizing our gifts and sharing them with the world. I imagine if we all tried to be a little more honest and vulnerable with our emotions, we would have more meaningful relationships and connections.

PUT YOURSELF FIRST

You might be thinking: How in the world can I put myself first? With so many demands and expectations, wouldn't it be nice to have such a luxury? I have often thought about this myself. Work deadlines, bills to pay, groceries to buy, caring for children, parents, lovers, and friends—even the dog gets fed and walked before I attend to my needs. Putting myself first is entirely counterintuitive to my personality, nature, and female conditioning. It took some dedicated introspection and journaling, but I learned how to set emotional and physical boundaries, allowing myself time to restore and engage in activities that brought me peace and joy. I hope this workbook will help you find that in your life.

MAKE TIME FOR YOU

It may feel impossible to make time for self-care. I found ways to sneak it into my daily routine by waking up 10 minutes early just to lie in bed and watch the sunrise, or allowing myself to listen to meditation music, uninterrupted, before going to bed. I take hot showers and practice focusing on the warm water and the smell of shampoo. I have prioritized going to the gym, even if I reward myself by watching a Netflix series uninterrupted while on the elliptical machine. Hey, whatever it takes, right? When my kids were small, I had to get a little more creative to find this time. The key in these smaller moments becomes making them count. Practicing mindfulness and staying present works best. I promise you that no one else will do it for you.

EVEN FIVE MINUTES IS BETTER THAN NOTHING

Self-nurturing opportunities happen all the time—a hot cup of tea, the smell of our soap, the sun on our face—and sometimes when we are preoccupied or lost in thought, we miss it. A trick to practicing self-love is to give yourself five minutes a day. Now during those five minutes, you must show up fully, staying present and aware. While five minutes may seem too short, it's not if you make it count. Practice being intentional, aware of every thought, feeling, and physical sensation without judgment. Those five minutes can help you connect with yourself and bring you peace of mind.

Five-Minute Self-Love Hacks

Here are three multisensory, self-soothing self-love hacks:

1. **Connect with nature and breathe.** Go outside and take a deep breath in through your nostrils and exhale through your mouth. Feel the sensation of your lungs filling with air and notice the calming effect on your body.

2. **Listen closely.** Close your eyes, paying attention to the sounds you hear around you. Just listen and notice without judging. There are no good or bad sounds. They just are. Now describe what you heard in your own words by sharing aloud or journaling. Just record the facts (for example, the clock ticked, the car door shut, the cat purred).

3. **Self-soothe through touch.** Practice soothing yourself physically in some way, perhaps by twirling your hair in your fingers, rubbing your arm gently, or massaging your neck. Notice the physical sensation and feeling of comfort. Sometimes we do this unconsciously and aren't even aware. Self-love must be intentional in the beginning, before it can become a habit. Practice physical touch with awareness and no judgment.

SCHEDULE IT SO YOU DON'T FORGET

Our lives are busy as we hustle around trying to complete the activities on our schedules. Often, we run out of time and energy by the end of the day, making self-love challenging to achieve. I have found that scheduling time to practice self-love makes a difference. If you're a morning person, maybe you can wake up 10 minutes earlier. If, like me, you can set aside lunchtime as a sacred time to refuel and cut out all distractions and demands, go ahead and do that. Sometimes we just need to schedule self-love practice into our busy lives and make it a priority. This is a great first step in the right direction.

SIMPLE WAYS TO PRACTICE
SELF-LOVE OUTSIDE OF THIS BOOK

There are many simple ways to practice self-love outside this work-book. I've listed a few here and I encourage you to explore the possibilities even further on your own. A list of helpful resources is included at the end of this book (page 153) to point you in the right direction.

MEDITATION

Meditation comes with many emotional, physical, and spiritual bene-fits. This practice helps manage stress and allows for a relaxation response within the body. When practicing meditation, the only thing that exists is in that moment. Meditation allows for creativity, new ideas, and sometimes a feeling of connectedness with something bigger than oneself. For some, meditation may have powerful spiritual implications. For others, it may allow for grounding and connected-ness with their physical body. Since meditation helps lower stress levels, it can become an essential component in managing chronic health issues like anxiety, chronic pain, insomnia, hypertension, inflammatory illnesses, tension headaches, and autoimmune disorders.

By offering ourselves the opportunity for stress reduction and taking time to reflect and re-center, we can shift focus from external events into our bodies—this is a form of self-love. By calming our minds and our bodies, we get in tune with ourselves.

One of my favorite ways to meditate involves turning down the lights and lighting a candle while asking my Alexa device to play relaxation and meditation music. I start with slow, deep breaths and focus on the sounds of the music. If a thought comes into my mind, I notice it and move it to an imaginary sticky note in the side of my mind to attend to later. Then I shift my focus back to my breathing and the music.

Of course, meditation does not have to happen at night, nor in a quiet bedroom. Once you get the hang of it you can practice anywhere, even when waiting for the subway, in line at the grocery store, or right before a big test.

VISUALIZATION

One of my favorite things to practice with clients is guided imagery meditation. After centering and calming through breath and focus, think of an image of something pleasing or calming. Then take a panoramic scan of the scene. The trick to effective visualization involves full sensory awareness. For a beach scene, it might be something like this:

> Picture being at the beach and focusing on the images and colors that you see. Perhaps it's a blue sky with white puffy clouds or blue-green water. Imagine the beach smells, such as the salty air or the smell of sunscreen. Imagine the taste of salt on your lips and the sounds of seagulls or waves crashing. Then feel the warm sun or cool beach breeze on your face. Start at the left and scan 180 degrees from left to right, noticing all of the colors and details that you might usually miss.

YOGA AND STRETCHING

Yoga and gentle stretching allow us to center and become grounded in our bodies. When we're stressed or anxious, our muscles tend to tighten up, becoming tense. This fight, flight, or freeze stress response sends chemicals and oxygen to our large muscle groups so we can respond to any real or perceived threat. Our bodies react the same way as if a scary animal chased us. In our modern life, we are not typically in physical or immediate danger, and we do not need these extra chemicals and oxygen. When we live in a state of pent-up stress, our bodies never get to discharge and release this built-up tension. Yoga and stretching assist in that release and become a way to treat our bodies kindly and with love. With yoga and stretching, the focus is on breathing, being present, and gently moving; not on burning calories or achieving demanding physical poses. When we stretch our muscles and center into our physical bodies, feelings of relaxation and rejuve-nation can emerge.

BREATHING

Perhaps one of the simplest, purest, and most effective ways to practice self-love involves intentional breathing. Of course, we breathe every day without thinking about it. But when we practice breathing as a method for stress management, we are showing ourselves love. As we quiet our minds and focus on our inhalations and exhalations, our bodies fill with life-sustaining oxygen, which gets transported throughout our bodies, right down to a cellular level. On an emotional level, breathing allows us to come into our bodies while focusing on the present moment. There are excellent apps that can prompt us to breathe correctly and intentionally, such as Calm and Headspace.

I prefer deep breathing from the diaphragm, called "belly breathing." By placing one hand on your chest and another on your stomach, you can tell if you are breathing correctly. The belly should move upward and out first, followed by the chest. Often when we are stressed or in a state of anxiety, breathing becomes shallow and from the chest. Slow and deep inhalations and exhalations trigger an immediate relaxation response. For an even more effective method, pair a one-word phrase or mantra with deep breathing. While inhaling, think, *I am good enough*, and while exhaling, breathe out any negative feelings or beliefs.

ADDITIONAL PRACTICES

Consider these simple self-love practices:

- **Journaling:** Put pen to paper, free-write without judgment, summarize feelings and daily events.

- **Self-love affirmations:** Read or say these aloud daily. I've included many sample affirmations throughout the book.

- **Set an alarm for 10 minutes before you have to get up:** Don't look at your phone—just lie there, savor your warm bed, and think gentle thoughts.

- **Hug yourself:** As you do, think loving thoughts about yourself, much as you would a dear friend.

Self-Assessment: How Do You Show Yourself Self-Love?

In this exercise, fill in the heart below with ways that you already show yourself love. Consider the different ways this happens. The first one can be that you are reading this workbook. If you have a hard time getting started, start by thinking of ways you show others love and see if any of those might apply to you.

Include the following:

1. Three ways you show your physical body love, such as nutritious food, a warm bath, and sleep.

2. Three ways that you engage in pleasing activities, such as hobbies, being outside with nature, or reading.

3. Three ways that you take time for yourself, such as waking up early for a cup of coffee, journaling, or limiting social media.

LET'S GET STARTED

Now that we've prepared for our trip in part 1, we are ready to take off! Part 2 of this workbook includes specific areas you can focus on during your self-love journey. You'll have opportunities to practice, journal, and assess yourself, as well as explore self-love even further. Remember that self-love evolves through intentional practice. While there may be days when it seems impossible to make the time or feel motivated, don't give up—these are often the most important days to press on. If you encounter a detour or make a pit stop, it's okay. Keep moving in the right direction. Remember that the journey is more important than reaching any particular destination. Self-love is an ever-evolving process.

CONCLUSION

We've got our map, vehicle, and supplies, and now we can start to embark on our self-love journey. Let's remind ourselves of what we've learned so far. Self-love involves purposeful practice. It requires vulnerability, honesty, and courage, but it does not mean we are perfect. Rather, self-love means we work toward finding our voices, our truths, and our authenticity through the practices of self-compassion and kindness.

I deserve to love myself.

"You have been criticizing yourself for years, and it hasn't worked. Try approving of yourself and see what happens."

—LOUISE L. HAY

PART TWO

Love Yourself More

Welcome to the second part of our workbook. Here's where the fun begins, as we begin to explore what's ahead. This next part involves delving deeper into understanding yourself and learning about your relationship with self-love through prompts, exercises, and experiential practice.

THREE

START WHERE YOU ARE

"A journey of a thousand miles begins with a single step."

—LAO-TZU

When you hear self-love, what comes to mind? For some women, self-love is a foreign concept. Some women struggle to feel worthy of even starting to learn to love themselves. Events such as early childhood trauma and growing up in invalidating environments can cause people to internalize the belief that their feelings and thoughts do not matter. Even just thinking about self-love sometimes triggers uncomfortable memories and emotions from the past. It may remind us of times when we felt unloved or received messages that we were not good enough. These shame-based messages can paralyze us, quickly shutting down our efforts to grow in self-love. It becomes essential for us to explore those fears and deeper blocks, as they may present barriers on our journeys. If strong feelings and memories become triggered in doing this work, you might find it immensely helpful to connect with a mental health provider, or get support from a trusted friend or loved one.

In this chapter, we will also evaluate where you are in your self-love journey and reflect on your goals for this workbook. These exercises are adaptable and can be used in any order that works for you.

LET'S SET SOME GOALS

1. What would I like to receive from this workbook (for example: personal growth, inner peace, self-confidence, healthier relationships)?

_____

_____

2. How will this look in my daily life (for example: "I will set aside 10 minutes every day to practice some form of self-love")?

_____

_____

3. When will I know that I have reached my goals?

_____

_____

4. What barriers might be present for me in practicing self-love (internal and external)?

_____

_____

5. Who can support me on my journey toward self-love (it's okay to include pets, too!)?

_____

_____

DIG A LITTLE DEEPER QUIZ

Let's dig a little deeper with the following quiz to learn more about where you stand with self-love. After each statement, circle the number that applies to you:

0 = never   **1** = rarely   **2** = sometimes   **3** = frequently
4 = most often   **5** = always

I believe that my feelings are valid.

0   1   2   3   4   5

I think my needs and wants are just as important as those of others.

0   1   2   3   4   5

I can effectively make requests or ask for what I need.

0   1   2   3   4   5

I enjoy spending time alone.

0   1   2   3   4   5

I can easily list five things I like about myself.

0   1   2   3   4   5

I do not say negative things to myself.

0   1   2   3   4   5

I talk to myself like I would my best friend or partner.

0   1   2   3   4   5

I like to take risks and go outside of my comfort zone.

0   1   2   3   4   5

I can make decisions that others might disagree with.

0   1   2   3   4   5

I take time to exercise several times a week.

0   1   2   3   4   5

I eat foods that help nourish my body.

0   1   2   3   4   5

I try new things and meet new people.

0   1   2   3   4   5

I am okay if someone disagrees with me.

0   1   2   3   4   5

I would be comfortable seeing a movie or eating at a sit-down restaurant alone.

0   1   2   3   4   5

Scoring:

Look over your responses to the statements in this quiz. Notice what numbers you tend to choose as a rating. Do you have mostly lower numbers (0–2) or higher numbers (3–5)? Which areas do you feel good about? Do you see any patterns or specific areas that you could develop, improve upon, or focus on throughout the workbook?

POWER TO WOMEN PLAYLIST

As a teenager, I used to love making mixtapes with some of my favorite songs. I recall one cassette (yes, cassette) I labeled "Power to Women." Why not make your own playlist of songs that inspire self-love—your own personal soundtrack? Try playing the music in the background while completing your workbook, or when you just need a pick-me-up. Music can be a powerful tool to inspire you and improve the moment.

Here are some possible fun songs to include in your playlist:

"I Will Survive" by Gloria Gaynor

"Fight Song" by Rachel Platten

"Girl On Fire" by Alicia Keys

"I'm Every Woman" by Chaka Khan

"Respect" by Aretha Franklin

"Beautiful" by Christina Aguilera

"Just Fine" by Mary J. Blige

"Born this Way" by Lady Gaga

"Juice," "Good as Hell," or others by Lizzo

"9 to 5" by Dolly Parton

Write down some songs for your power playlist here:

1. _____
2. _____
3. _____
4. _____
5. _____
6. _____
7. _____
8. _____
9. _____
10. _____

AFFIRM ME

Affirmations can be an excellent tool to start training your mind to think positive thoughts about yourself. They work best when they are simple, believable, and relatable. They also may feel awkward to say at first—but with practice, you are cementing the message into your psyche. What you say becomes your truth. Look into the mirror every morning and try saying at least one affirmation aloud. Here are a few examples that you can use as practice. Even better, add your personalized affirmations in the blank spaces below.

I am worthy of love and belonging.

Loving myself is as important as loving others.

It is okay to ask for what I need and want.

My feelings are valid. There is no right or wrong way to feel.

I can get my needs met and not feel selfish.

_____

_____

_____

_____

FEELING UNWORTHY

Think back to the earliest time you struggled with feeling unworthy. Describe your experience in the space provided. Feeling creative? You can even draw a picture of the situation in the box.

_____

_____

_____

_____

_____

_____

_____

SELF-LOVE HAPPENS

Describe a time when you recently experienced self-love. What was happening? What thoughts did you have about yourself? What did it feel like to have these positive feelings toward yourself?

_____

_____

_____

_____

_____

A MESSAGE FOR YOUR YOUNGER SELF

If you had to talk to a younger version of yourself, what would you say to her? Would you tell her not to worry so much about what everyone else thought and focus more on things that mattered to her? Fill in the conversation bubble below with what you would say.

INTERNALIZED CRITICAL VOICE

Share any negative beliefs you have internalized that make practicing self-love difficult. These beliefs may come from your childhood, family of origin, societal messages, and romantic relationships. Write each belief in a cloud below.

For example: "If I don't get the promotion at work, I am not good enough."

FIVE POSITIVE MESSAGES

In the space provided, identify five positive messages about yourself that you have received from others. These may have helped you feel more confident or worthy, or you may not have even believed them. While it's not necessary to fully believe them at this point, perhaps these messages can serve as a launching pad to finding self-worth. If you have trouble with this section, feel free to ask a friend or loved one to share what they consider to be your positive qualities.

1. _____

_____

2. _____

_____

3. _____

_____

4. _____

_____

5. _____

_____

RECOGNIZE YOUR INSECURITIES

What kinds of situations make it hard to feel good about yourself? Color in those shapes. Add your own examples in the blank spots.

Meeting someone new

Online dating

Eating in front of someone

Wearing a bathing suit

Flipping through a magazine

HURDLES TO LOVING YOURSELF

As a society, we have made great strides in equality, thanks in part to the women's movement. Still, societal messages continue to impact our self-worth. Think about how you feel after looking at magazine ads, airbrushed models, and the portrayal of women in movies, music videos, and even toys like Barbie dolls. List some of the faulty messages that you receive from societal beliefs and perceived standards for women (I have listed a few to get you started).

For example: A woman must look good at all times.
For example: Wrinkles and cellulite are unattractive.

1. _____
   _____

2. _____
   _____

3. _____
   _____

4. _____
   _____

5. _____
   _____

BATHING SUIT BLUES

Take a moment to close your eyes and visualize yourself in a bathing suit at the pool or beach. How do you feel about your body? Are you tempted to compare yourself to others? What body parts cause you self-consciousness? What body parts do you love? Use the space below to share your feelings and thoughts about your body and how you value it.

_____

_____

_____

_____

_____

Refocus Your Attention

Body image is a powerful influencer of how we feel about ourselves, but you can learn to accept and even love your body. Here's a simple, effective, and powerful method to refocus your thoughts. Whether you're at the beach or a pool, focus your energy on the experience—whether that involves boogie boarding, reading, looking for sharks' teeth, or beating your kids at four-square. Rather than obsessively focusing on your body, choose to pay attention to the sensory experience and all the fun ways you can move your body and enjoy the atmosphere. What can you see, smell, taste, touch, and hear? Think about other places or situations that create feelings of insecurity. Try refocusing your attention on the full sensory experience so you can live fully in that moment and lose self-consciousness.

GET TO KNOW YOURSELF

Part of self-love work involves getting to truly know yourself at your core—understanding your values and what is important to you. In the space provided, write words, draw pictures, or even cut and paste pictures and words from magazines that bring joy, peace, curiosity, and excitement to your life. Think about hobbies, favorite seasons, memories of good times, etc. As a bonus, you will have a better awareness and a visual representation of what makes you uniquely you.

GIFTS, STRENGTHS, AND TALENTS, OH MY!

Part of self-love involves recognizing our inherent gifts and strengths. Make a list of at least five of your gifts, talents, and strengths. Don't just list the roles you have in life, like mother, friend, daughter, wife, etc. Instead, think about what makes you valuable in these roles, and more important, as an individual. What traits are you the proudest of? For example, think about your sense of humor, how hardworking you are, or your ability to connect with those around you.

1. _____

_____

2. _____

_____

3. _____

_____

4. _____

_____

5. _____

_____

WHAT MOTIVATES ME?

It can feel challenging to stay motivated when you're starting something new. In the space provided, share what makes you want to work on loving yourself more. Keep this list handy for when you have a rough day and feel like giving up on this workbook.

_____

_____

_____

_____

_____

PERSONALITY INVENTORY

A transformative component of practicing self-love is learning more about yourself. If you prefer being alone rather than going to parties, or you would rather work out at home than join a class, or possess other traits that you question, please know that your personality is your unique chemistry—embrace it. Once I learned about my personality type, my self-love strengthened. I now accept my personality without judgment, and so can you. Check out the resources at the end of the book (page 153) for links to websites to find your personality type and record your results here:

My 16Personalities.com or Myers-Briggs Personality Inventory Results: _____

My Enneagram Type:

_____

A GUIDED MEDITATION FOR HEALING

In this exercise, we will enjoy a guided imagery meditation that focuses on self-love.

1. Sit comfortably in a quiet place and allow yourself to notice your breathing. Slowly inhale for a count of four, hold your breath for a count of four, and exhale for a count of four.

2. Repeat several times, pausing in between, and allow your body to become more settled. Feel free to shift your sitting position to get more comfortable.

3. Now picture a color that you find calming and soothing. Imagine inhaling this color through your nose as a mist. Let this colored mist swirl throughout your body, starting with your head.

4. Allow the mist to work down your chest and throughout your core. Let the mist trickle down your limbs to your fingers and toes. Allow the colored mist to resonate and vibrate throughout each little part of your body, bathing you in a healing and loving light.

5. Picture this mist swirling around and centering at your heart as it becomes more concentrated in color. Feel the warmth and allow this mist to envelop you in self-love and healing. Notice now how this feels to you.

6. Continue this breathing for a few minutes or for as long as you wish.

THESE ARE A FEW OF MY FAVORITE THINGS

Part of loving yourself is getting to know what you like and do not like. Let's make a list of your current favorite things:

Favorite sweet treat: _____

Favorite drink: _____

Favorite sport: _____

Favorite place to be: _____

Favorite person: _____

Favorite hobby: _____

Favorite time of day: _____

Favorite salty snack: _____

Favorite book: _____

Favorite movie or TV show: _____

Sticky Note Reminders

For this quick and easy practice tip, you will need five sticky notes and your favorite pen or marker. Write down five quick, straightforward messages that can help remind you of your worth and prompt you to practice self-love. Here are some ideas if you need help:

- I am worthy of love and belonging.
- I am learning to love myself every day.
- Self-love is a journey. I'm ready to start now!
- I can learn self-love by paying attention to what I think is important.
- My feelings and thoughts matter.

Put these notes on your mirror, in a notebook, or any place you will see them whenever you need a reminder of your self-worth.

CONCLUSION

By now, I'm sure you realize self-love takes time and effort. But with that work comes the potential for incredible life changes. As you complete the exercises in the workbook, you will gain a better understanding of what self-love means and in which areas you could grow more. Part of practicing self-love involves appreciation and gratitude. As we begin the next section, try telling yourself how proud you are of yourself for starting this self-love journey and workbook. By doing this, you can launch into the next chapter on self-compassion with a positive mindset.

I wholeheartedly love myself, flaws and all.

FOUR
FIND SELF-COMPASSION

"Whenever I notice something about myself I don't like, or whenever something goes wrong in my life, I silently repeat the following phrases: This is a moment of suffering. Suffering is part of life. May I be kind to myself in this moment. May I give myself the compassion I need."

—KRISTEN NEFF

Self-compassion centers around practicing kindness and respect toward ourselves. It also requires openness and vulnerability in acknowledging past trauma or mistakes and working through difficult emotions like anger, hurt, and sadness. Self-compassion allows us to release criticism and self-judgment.

It is essential to differentiate self-compassion from self-esteem Often, as we go through life, we learn to focus on feeling good about ourselves based on our accomplishments and positive qualities. However, in moments of suffering, self-compassion outshines self-esteem. With self-compassion, our worth is not dependent on the outcome. A self-compassionate response cuts through extreme beliefs, normalizes the feeling, and offers encouragement through the disappointment.

WHAT WOULD I TELL A FRIEND?

Internalized messages from past traumatic events or childhood wounds may contribute to feelings of unworthiness, making practicing self-compassion challenging. The quickest way to create a self-compassionate response involves thinking about how you might respond to a beloved friend.

In the following situations, write what you would say to a friend to help them feel better:

1. I just got fired from my job for making a mistake.

_____

_____

2. My significant other broke up with me.

_____

_____

3. I did not get hired for my dream job because I was underqualified.

_____

_____

4. My friends had a party and didn't invite me.

_____

_____

5. I had to go up a dress size.

_____

_____

SOCIAL MEDIA CLEAN-UP

Have you ever noticed how you feel about yourself after browsing social media? Many of us feel worse after scrolling through Facebook or Instagram. This change in self-worth can come from comparing ourselves to others. Make a list of your social media accounts and ask yourself these questions: Do I feel empowered, good enough, and happy after being on this social media site? Jot down a few notes about how each of these sites make you feel, and cross off any sites that make you feel worse. Consider adjusting the feeds or unfollowing people to only allow for pictures and messages that inspire, nurture, and empower. Taking this action can become a big step toward practicing and discovering self-love and self-compassion.

1. _____

_____

2. _____

_____

3. _____

_____

4. _____

_____

5. _____

_____

A LETTER TO MY YOUNGER SELF

Think back to a time in your life when you struggled and faced disappointment, rejection, or failure. Perhaps it was trying out for a part in the school play, facing a breakup in a relationship, or not getting the job you wanted. Fill in the blanks to this guided self-compassion letter to yourself.

Dear _____ ,
(YOUR NAME HERE)

I hope you know that when _____
(INSERT SITUATION)

_____ ,

I was in your corner rooting for you. People sometimes go through tough times and

this time was hard because _____
(DESCRIBE WHAT WAS DIFFICULT ABOUT THIS)

_____ **. It's okay and normal to feel** _____
(STATE HOW YOU FELT AT THE TIME)

_____ .

I want you to know that it is okay because _____
(WHY IS THIS GOING TO BE OKAY?)

_____ **. Sometimes you are just too hard on yourself. I know**

you will get through this because _____
(DESCRIBE HOW YOU GOT THROUGH IT)

_____ **. Never forget your amazing qualities like**

(LIST YOUR AMAZING QUALITIES. SEE PAGE 37 FOR A REMINDER)

_____ **. I always love**

you and know that you will get through this.

Yours truly,

_____
(YOUR NAME HERE)

COMPASSIONATE COMEBACKS

Part of self-compassion involves challenging negative beliefs and silencing your inner critic. For each of the following negative statements, see if you can come up with a kinder, gentler self-statement.

I am never good enough. _____

No one will ever love me. _____

I can't do anything right. _____

I am so stupid. _____

Why can't I do this correctly? _____

I am a loser. _____

PRACTICE MAKES PERMANENT (NOT PERFECT)

Self-compassion and kindness can go a long way when you are learning something new like how to ride a bike, drive a car, or cook a new dish. It is okay to make mistakes and keep trying as part of the process of learning. Think about a time you tried something new. What did you tell yourself to encourage yourself not to give up? What did you do to improve?

_____

_____

_____

_____

_____

A MEDITATION FOR WORKING THROUGH UNCOMFORTABLE FEELINGS

Some emotions can be uncomfortable and hard to experience. We often try to make them go away or tell ourselves that we should not have them. Unfortunately, suppressing feelings can lead to many other problems, including health issues, relationship challenges, and numbing behaviors. Part of self-compassion involves allowing yourself to experience the full range of emotions.

For this exercise:

1. Close your eyes and practice mindfully breathing.

2. Allow yourself to become calmer with each inhalation and exhalation.

3. Notice any uncomfortable feelings you have experienced recently. They could include shame, fear, boredom, rejection, or something else.

4. Think about where you experience this feeling in your body.

5. When you encounter this emotion, kindly remind yourself that your feelings are natural and that it is okay to honor them with compassion.

6. When you are ready, take a deep breath and open your eyes.

WE'RE ALL IN THIS TOGETHER

Dr. Kristen Neff is a leading psychologist and an expert on self-compassion. Part of her research involves identifying an essential component of self-compassion. She explains that suffering is part of the human condition. We all suffer and struggle, and this contributes to a sense of humanity. This exercise can help us realize we are not alone in our challenges. Circle the universal human struggles and challenges that you have experienced so far in your life.

Death of a
loved one

Telling a joke
and no
one laughs

Breaking
something
important

Doing poorly
on a test

Quarantine
due to a pandemic

Losing a
friendship

Being alone

Feeling
left out

Losing something
valuable (like
your purse)

Breakup of
a relationship

Gaining
weight

SPEAK KINDLY TO YOURSELF

Children are so wonderful and innocent and pure. Have you ever thought about how you speak to a child? Stop and think about it— you would never speak to a child the way you may sometimes talk to yourself. In this exercise, write down some common self-talk statements and see if you can adapt them to sound more compassionate, like you would say them to a child.

Example: "I am such an idiot." (after dropping my phone)

Answer: It's okay, it didn't break. I'm sure I'm not the first person to drop a phone.

Statement: _____

_____

Answer: _____

_____

Statement: _____

_____

Answer: _____

_____

Statement: _____

_____

Answer: _____

_____

MANTRAS FOR SELF-COMPASSION

Mantras and affirmations can help reinforce self-compassion. See which ones listed here resonate with you. Try saying these or posting them where you can read them daily. Feel free to add your own on the lines below:

- I am doing the best that I can right now, and that is enough.

- I am worthy, even when I struggle.

- I can allow myself to feel all my emotions, even uncomfortable ones.

- My feelings are neither good nor bad. They just are.

- My thoughts are just thoughts.

- I can make mistakes. They are a normal part of growing and learning.

- I pay attention to my body and how it feels.

- I am learning and growing every day.

- What is important to me might differ from what is important to someone else. And that's okay.

- I can handle it if not everyone likes me.

_____

_____

_____

SELF-ESTEEM VS. SELF-COMPASSION

We talked earlier about the differences between self-compassion and self-esteem. Self-compassion allows us to be kind to ourselves even when we struggle, while self-esteem reflects how we feel about ourselves in relation to our accomplishments. If you were looking at a chart comparing the two, your self-compassion would stay steady no matter what the circumstance, while self-esteem would go up and down depending on how your ego felt. Think about the differences in each situation below, and notice how much more helpful the self-compassionate responses are.

Example: Got a raise

Self-compassion response: *I have worked hard for this and I deserve it.*
Self-esteem response: *I am the best. Everyone will know that I am great!*

Forgot an important meeting

Self-compassion response: _____

Self-esteem response: _____

Asked out on a date

Self-compassion response: _____

Self-esteem response: _____

Friend declined my invite

Self-compassion response: _____

Self-esteem response: _____

HOW YOU GOT HERE

The classic children's book *The Velveteen Rabbit* by Margery Williams Bianco contains a dialogue between the Skin Horse and the child, in which the Skin Horse shares what it means to be real. He describes being worn down by his loving owner, and how he doesn't mind being worn down, even if it means his eyes drop out or his hair gets worn off from petting.

I have always loved this metaphor for life. By experiencing and surviving life, even its painful events and suffering, we become more beautiful and complete. This passage rings true for self-compassion as well. In the space provided, share both positive and challenging situations that have shaped who you have become and have taught you more about being real.

Positive Situations

- _____
  _____
- _____
  _____
- _____
  _____
- _____
  _____
- _____
  _____

Challenging Situations

- _____
  _____
- _____
  _____
- _____
  _____
- _____
  _____
- _____
  _____

SELF-COMPASSION QUIZ

Answer the following true or false questions by circling the response that feels most accurate for you.

1. **I allow myself to make mistakes and see them as learning opportunities.**

   True   False

2. **I allow myself to experience all my emotions.**

   True   False

3. **When I'm lonely, I will beat myself up and tell myself that no one likes me.**

   True   False

4. **Speaking harshly to myself is an effective way of motivating myself to do better.**

   True   False

5. **If I fail, I believe I am not good enough.**

   True   False

6. **Struggling and suffering are a part of the human experience.**

   True   False

7. **I punish myself for making mistakes.**

   True   False

8. **I must be perfect to be loved or good enough.**

   True   False

9. **I am as kind to myself as I am to other people.**

   True   False

10. **I tend to overreact to my feelings and exaggerate my response to get validation.**

    True   False

Scoring:

Give yourself 5 points for every TRUE answer for questions 1, 2, 6, and 9. Give yourself 5 points for every FALSE answer for questions 3, 4, 5, 7, 8, and 10.

90–100: You are a self-compassion queen! Keep up the fantastic work in loving and being kind to yourself.

80–90: Keep it up! You are on your way to practicing self-compassion daily.

70–80: Continue to challenge yourself to be kinder and more encouraging to yourself.

60–70: Keep learning, and remember that everyone struggles with hard times. This understanding is an essential aspect of practicing self-compassion.

50–60: Keep practicing. Self-compassion may be a new way of experiencing life. Allow yourself to notice your feelings and talk to yourself in a kind and loving manner.

0–50: Let's try some self-compassion right now! You are taking steps to grow and become more loving and forgiving to yourself. Remember, the three components to self-compassion involve being kind to yourself, recognizing the humanity in struggles, and practicing mindfulness.

HARDEST LESSONS

What situations and experiences have you gone through that proved challenging to show self-compassion? Share an experience here, and describe what helped you overcome and get through the difficult time.

_____

_____

_____

_____

_____

_____

_____

_____

Voice-Changer Hack

On days when you're feeling down or struggling to find any inkling of self-compassion, I have a secret hack that might help. I came up with this in a therapy session and must admit I use it myself now. I have a voice changer app on my phone that allows me to record a statement and then play it back in different types of voices. First, I record myself saying the negative self-talk statement. For instance, "I'm not good enough." Then I play this back over and over, using the different voice sounds. It becomes a great way to defuse the negative thought and become less stuck to the meaning. My favorite voices are the Robot, Alien, and Chipmunk. Alternatively, you can simply use your own voice and say these statements in a funny way—try saying them like a robot or even Mickey Mouse! It's hard to stay so serious and negative when something makes you laugh or smile.

ALLOW FOR YOUR FEELINGS

Mindfulness can help us work toward self-compassion. As we have discussed, mindfulness means observing the present moment without judgment. Judgment is when we tell ourselves that what we're doing or feeling is right or wrong, or good or bad. It's the *should*s and *shouldn't*s. Some emotions can feel overwhelming or uncomfortable, causing us to want to suppress or numb ourselves. You can practice noticing emotions by first recognizing what happens in your body in conjunction with your different feelings.

Example: Anger: My body becomes tense, my face gets hot, I clench my teeth.

Sadness: _____

Fear: _____

Joy: _____

Disgust: _____

Surprise: _____

FEEL YOUR FEELINGS

Feelings are neither good nor bad. They are just like waves in the ocean—they come and go. However, when we try to fight them, it can feel a little like drowning. Try instead to surf your feelings or float with them. They will pass, and new ones will come. List all the feelings you have already experienced today, and consider how they came and went.

_____

_____

_____

PERFECTLY IMPERFECT

As humans, we are all flawed and imperfect. The acceptance of this belief is a critical component of understanding and practicing self-compassion. After establishing mindfulness and learning to experience our feelings and thoughts nonjudgmentally, self-compassion goes even further. It requires genuine kindness and acceptance of our flaws and imperfections with grace and compassion, not just awareness. Make a list here of five shortcomings and remind yourself that you are perfectly imperfect in the column beside it.

Example: I am messy and leave crumbs on the floor.

It's okay to be messy.

1. _____

2. _____

3. _____

4. _____

5. _____

1. _____

2. _____

3. _____

4. _____

5. _____

EMBRACE HUMOR

Humor can be an excellent way to defuse and let go of negative self-talk. In the square provided, design a meme or cartoon about how you are self-compassionate using a picture from a magazine, or even one you draw. Sometimes a little humor can make heavy situations feel lighter.

LET NEGATIVE THOUGHTS FLOAT BY

Wouldn't it be nice if we could just delete negative thoughts? Perhaps you can visualize a silly way to pop or zap negative thoughts about yourself that come to mind. Think of words as balloons that you can let float on by out of your mind. Tell yourself, "There is that negative word. Just notice it and let it go." Now think of a statement like "I'm never good enough" and practice observing and dismissing the negative self-talk or internalized critical voices.

Self-Compassion Tips

In addition to what we've explored in this chapter, here are a few more quick and easy tips for embracing self-compassion when you need it:

- Next time you feel negative self-talk coming on, give yourself a big squeeze.
- Tell yourself what you would tell a good friend—*you're only human and you're awesome.*
- Give yourself a break—step away from what you're doing. Move into another space, like nature, or your favorite corner of your home, relax your body, and breathe.
- Make an affirmation jar. Fill it with messages to yourself that remind you what is special and great about you. Pull them out as needed.
- Conversely, write down negative self-talk statements and then throw them away in a symbolic gesture of release.
- Seek out the people and pets that make you feel good.
- Take a break from social media and unplug from electronics. Quiet your world and reflect on what is around you.
- Do something just for the fun of it. Create, bake, paint, write, color— whatever lifts you up.

CONCLUSION

I hope this chapter has been helpful and filled with tools you can use for self-compassion. Navigating vulnerable and uncomfortable places, especially from our pasts, can be challenging. By adding self-compassion to the mix, we change the game dramatically. No matter what obstacles and detours come our way, self-compassion allows us to keep moving forward. In the next chapter, we will explore self-doubt and those nagging, internal voices that cause us to not believe in ourselves. Self-compassion will surely come in handy in the next leg of our journey.

Loving myself means embracing
and learning from my mistakes.

FIVE
RELEASE SELF-DOUBT

"The future belongs to those who believe in the beauty of their dreams."

—ELEANOR ROOSEVELT

Sometimes, our greatest adversary in life lives within the walls of our own minds. By replaying past events and life challenges from a critical space, our heads become filled with self-doubt and insecurities. The problem lies in these thought patterns leading us to self-sabotage our relationships, healthy behaviors, and efforts to achieve personal fulfillment. In this chapter, our self-love journey involves establishing a strong foundation on which to build self-worth. The first step requires us to learn ways to release internalized and life-limiting beliefs from past events and relationships. We will create a strong foundation by tearing down others' views of us and freeing space to build up with our gifts and talents.

In working toward creating self-love, it's essential to challenge and release negative thoughts and beliefs about ourselves. The following exercises provide an opportunity to gain more insight and awareness into the origins of self-love. These activities will also offer practical tips and practices to learn strategies and skills to release negative and self-limiting beliefs.

SELF-DOUBT QUIZ

Complete this short quiz to see how self-doubt may have limited your life. Give yourself 10 points for every answer of "true."

1. **I do not like to try something new unless I am good at it.**

   True   False

2. **I am often afraid of making mistakes.**

   True   False

3. **I often believe that I am not good enough.**

   True   False

4. **I am afraid to go outside my comfort zone.**

   True   False

5. **I believe that others will not like me.**

   True   False

6. **I replay conversations and think of things I could have said better.**

   True   False

7. **I do not like to try new things.**

   True   False

8. **I worry about what others will think of me.**

   True   False

9. **I believe I have failed many times.**

   True   False

10. **I often think negative, catastrophic thoughts that start with "What if..."**

    True   False

Scoring:

0–40: You have done fantastic work on treating yourself kindly and encouraging yourself. Keep it up. Your world is a better place because you live fully and wholeheartedly.

40–60: There are some situations in which you struggle to feel worthy, and other times, you are comfortable with yourself. Continue to recognize and challenge your inner critical voice.

60–80: You often hold back from living fully due to fears and insecurities. Keep working and practicing to build your confidence and achieve the things you deserve.

80–100: You are in the right place by reading this book. It's great that you are recognizing how crucial conquering self-doubt can be in improving yourself and your life.

SELF-DOUBT THOUGHT BUBBLE

Think about a situation that brings you feelings of self-doubt. Perhaps it is a public speaking presentation, a sports game, or a first date. Notice what thoughts might come to mind and record them in the thought bubble. After identifying the negative thought, try not to focus on whether it is true or untrue, but instead whether it is helpful to your self-love journey. If not, try creating a new view that supports self-love and kindness. Practice saying that new view to yourself aloud five times.

POSITIVE MEMORIES

Imagine a time in your life when you felt confident and secure with yourself. In the space provided, describe the situation and what you experienced. Remember what this felt like in your body and how you presented yourself to the outside world. What was it about this situation that helped you feel confident and secure?

_____

_____

_____

_____

"WHAT IF" BUSTERS

Most worry thoughts begin with the words "What if." Self-doubt presents us with similar beliefs. *What if I look stupid? What if I fail? What if I don't get the job?* The next time you catch yourself thinking, "What if," try to complete the sentence with the opposite of your fear. Notice how this converse thinking leads to more positive feelings. If you struggle to believe the complete opposite, try to at least find a neutral response. Complete the following "What if" statements using this method.

Example: What if I fail?   What if I succeed?

What if I lose? _____   **What if . . .** _____

_____   _____

What if they don't like me? _____   **What if . . .** _____

_____   _____

What if I'm not pretty enough? _____   **What if . . .** _____

_____   _____

What if I look or sound stupid? _____   **What if . . .** _____

_____   _____

What if . . . _____   **What if . . .** _____

_____   _____

What if . . . _____   **What if . . .** _____

_____   _____

What if . . . _____   **What if . . .** _____

_____   _____

BODY LANGUAGE MAKES A DIFFERENCE

Picture how a person stands when feeling confident and secure. What do you notice? Now, picture a person who feels insecure and has self-doubt. What do you see is different? The following exercise can help you consider how body language can impact our feelings about ourselves. Even when you are not feeling confident, you can take a deep breath, make sure your feet are solidly on the floor, straighten your back, let your arms relax at your sides, and soften your facial muscles. Try standing up straight, and the feelings will come. After taking on a confident stance, write down the three confident body markers that feel most natural to you. Follow this by listing some insecure body markers.

Confident Body Language

_____

_____

_____

_____

_____

_____

_____

_____

_____

_____

Insecure Body Language

_____

_____

_____

_____

_____

_____

_____

_____

_____

_____

MY PROUDEST MOMENTS

In the following exercise, list your top five accomplishments and things that make you feel the proudest about the past year. These items do not have to be what others might view as success. Consider anything that makes you feel proud, including overcoming something challenging. These triumphs and small wins are often the sweetest rewards.

1. _____

2. _____

3. _____

4. _____

5. _____

MY CHEERLEADING TEAM

Sometimes in life, it helps to have a cheerleading team filled with people who love and support us. Who have your cheerleaders been? Perhaps they played only a small role in your life. I recall my second-grade teacher was someone who encouraged and believed in me, even though she was one of the toughest teachers I had. Her faith in me helped me gain confidence when I was a shy and anxious child. List the cheerleaders that you have had in your life and think about their impact on you.

1. _____

2. _____

3. _____

4. _____

5. _____

INHALE CONFIDENCE, EXHALE SELF-DOUBT

Deep breathing, paired with one or two words, provides a powerful way to center and become grounded. Begin by finding a comfortable and quiet place to sit. Consider lighting a candle, dimming the lights, or playing some soothing music. Next, follow the steps to practice guided breathing for as long as comfortable. When first starting, you might find this exercise difficult. Start by timing yourself for a minute and see if you can focus for that long. If you are just starting with breathing exercises and find that this is too long, even practicing for a minute can prove helpful.

1. Take a deep inhale through your nose or mouth for a count of 4 seconds, filling your belly and then your chest with air.

2. Hold your breath for a count of 4 seconds. Slowly exhale through the mouth for a count of 4 seconds. Repeat this breathing sequence and add the final steps.

3. As you breathe in, pick a word or two words that represent how you would like to feel about yourself. Perhaps it's "I've got this" or "Confidence."

4. As you exhale, release all self-doubt and insecurities. Repeat this exercise for a minute or for as long as you feel comfortable. Try to lengthen the amount of time as you progress.

SELF-DOUBT MOUNTAIN

For this exercise, think of one big goal you have and write it inside the mountain. Then, think of things that hold you back as you work toward that goal. Write these obstacles in the arrows—you can choose from the following list or create your own. As you commit to not letting these obstacles hold you back, you'll reach new heights!

Possible obstacles:

- What others think

- Past failures

- Rejection

- The odds are slim

- Not everybody can do it

- I realize I'm taking a risk

SELF-DOUBT BUSTERS

Think about situations that cause you the most self-doubt. What do you notice about your negative thoughts? Answer the following questions to challenge and bust through the self-doubt:

1. **What would I tell a friend who had this same negative belief?**

   _____

   _____

   _____

2. **If I were kind to myself, how would I change this thought?**

   _____

   _____

   _____

3. **What would be a more helpful thought to have?**

   _____

   _____

   _____

4. **What evidence is there that this negative belief is true? What evidence is there that it is untrue?**

   _____

   _____

   _____

WHAT WOULD A FRIEND TELL ME?

Imagine that someone who loves and appreciates you is sitting next to you after a particularly challenging day when your self-doubts are running high. Explain the challenging situation on the lines below and then fill in the speaking bubble with what your supportive person might say to remind you how awesome and amazing you are.

_____

_____

_____

_____

_____

_____

TAKE AN AFFIRMING WALK

Sometimes we might hear or say encouraging and helpful things to ourselves, but still have a hard time believing they are true. We might even know them in our heads, but not connect with them in our hearts. Repeating positive phrases or mantras aloud until they become your internal voice may help. Circle the mantra that fits best for you or come up with your own, and repeat it to yourself as you take a walk for 10 or 15 minutes.

I've got this.

I will figure it out.

I am good enough.

It's okay.

I have talents and gifts.

I will do great.

It will all work out.

I am prepared.

I have a lot to offer.

They are lucky to have me.

People like and want to be around me.

I can do it!

In the grand scheme of life . . .

I am capable.

I am honest, smart, funny.

IT'S OKAY TO . . .

Some of my favorite children's books are part of a series by Todd Parr. His books often share the simple message that "it's okay" to be different, make mistakes, be sad, etc. In the space provided, share situations or feelings that you believe are okay, even if they feel uncomfortable. You might say, "It's okay to make a mistake," or "It's okay to change your mind." What are your "okays"?

It's okay _____

It's okay _____

It's okay _____

It's okay _____

It's okay _____

POSITIVE PEOPLE

Think about a positive and supportive person whom you have encountered in your life. Perhaps a coach, mentor, teacher, or family member. What qualities did they show that helped inspire you? Were they confident, self-assured, authentic, clear-headed, wise, or something else? Think about ways you are like or can be more like this person, and list them in the space provided.

_____

_____

_____

_____

_____

REFRAME, REFRAME, REFRAME

As a therapist, I often use reframing as a technique to help someone try to look at their situation differently. This technique helps adjust negative interpretations of events to find a positive spin. Here are some examples of situations that could use some reframing. Try it on yourself and see what it's like:

Example: This event is too hard. Reframe: I am learning to keep going even when it's hard.

Example: I hate social distancing. Reframe: I get to spend more quality time with myself.

I will never be good enough. _____

_____

I am lazy. _____

_____

I never get to do what I want. _____

_____

A Mindfulness Hack

Mindfulness involves observing and noticing without judgment. The next time you find yourself struggling with self-doubt or insecurity, pay attention to your thoughts. Become an observer of what your critical voice is telling you. Notice how a thought is just a thought—nothing more, nothing less. When you observe a thought, it allows you to take a step away from the actual belief. I often say it enables us to look at the tornado from the outside instead of being swept up and spun around. For the next five minutes, try to notice what thoughts come and go in your mind without changing or fixing them, and without getting sucked up into the thought.

WHO SHAPED YOUR CRITICAL VOICE?

Take a moment to reflect on and identify any people or events that may have helped create the internalized critical voice that you hear in your head. Think back to situations that might have stood out as defining moments in your development. For instance, a client shared her memory of answering a math question incorrectly in grade school. She recalled feeling embarrassed as the class laughed at her. This moment resulted in a lifelong belief that she was "not good" at math.

Person or Event	Message

FAMILY OF ORIGIN MYTHS

Often in families, some passed-on myths, beliefs, and mottos can be harmful even when they're meant to encourage. In my family, we believed in the army motto, "Be All That You Can Be." While it was meant to inspire and motivate us to do our best, I often found myself doing everything possible to be *the* best. So much so that I became the worst version of myself! Clearly, I took this motto to the extreme. What are some of your childhood family myths or beliefs? Do they work for who you are today?

_____

_____

_____

_____

_____

Observe and Release Your Thoughts

We can become glued to a negative thought by merely trying to prove or disprove the belief. Even by challenging the notion, we think about the thought even more. The next time you have a negative thought, instead of trying to make it go away or change it, try finding a more helpful thought and start paying attention to that one. Using the mindfulness skills you have been practicing, notice and allow the unhelpful thought to simply be while you add a new and better thought that is more helpful to focus on. For ideas, consider the exercises you have already completed. Pick a thought that supports your self-love journey—one that helps you feel more compassionate and kinder to yourself, and that can shift your focus away from self-doubt.

A LOVE LETTER TO MYSELF

In this exercise, write a love letter to yourself. Include things that you appreciate about yourself. Point out your gifts and talents. Think about things that others have complimented you on, or how you have overcome challenges. You can reread this letter on days when you have high levels of self-doubt and need a reminder of your awesomeness. You might even choose to make a copy to carry with you, or keep on your dresser or nightstand for a quick reminder of your goodness and worth.

Dear _____,
(YOUR NAME HERE)

_____

_____

_____

_____

_____

_____

_____

_____

_____

_____

_____

_____

_____

Love,

_____
(YOUR NAME HERE)

CONCLUSION

Every journey toward self-love will certainly have speed bumps and potholes filled with self-doubt. When we release these negative messages, we feel empowered and gain freedom from limiting, entrenched beliefs. Often stemming from childhood wounds, unhealthy relationships, and negative messages in the world around us, these limiting beliefs can change us by creating insecurities and internalized messages that we are not good enough. Releasing self-doubt is an act of self-love. Congratulate yourself for allowing yourself to be vulnerable and doing the hard work to free yourself from old and entrenched messages. Now comes the exciting part, where we build a stronger foundation for self-love, comprised of self-worth, boundaries, and recognition of our strengths.

Loving myself starts with taking care of me.

SIX

BUILD YOUR SELF-WORTH

"I will go on adventuring, changing, opening my mind and my eyes, refusing to be stamped and stereotyped. The thing is to free one's self: to let it find its dimensions, not be impeded."

—VIRGINIA WOOLF

By releasing self-doubt, we become free to fill up that space with self-worth. Building self-worth is like building a house. To start, we need the right tools and a strong foundation. As we let go of self-doubt and insecurities, we are able to build on solid ground. Tools for increasing confidence include positive self-talk, recognition of our gifts and strengths, and the ability to love and appreciate our whole selves, including our bodies, hearts, and minds. This chapter will also focus on body image, as many women struggle to accept and love their bodies.

PLANT YOUR SELF-WORTH GARDEN

Before building self-worth, it is essential to figure out which seeds you'll need to plant for your garden to flourish. On the seed packets below, mark which seeds you find most important to grow your self-worth. Feel free to add your own seeds on the lines below!

Kind Self-Talk   Positive Thoughts   Making Time for Myself   Trying New Things   Making the Effort   Body Positivity

Pick Your Own

_____

_____

Pick Your Own

_____

_____

Pick Your Own

_____

_____

Soft and Loving Eyes Trick

One helpful trick when you find yourself feeling critical and negative about yourself and your body is to notice your eyes. When we're feeling critical, our eyes become smaller and more laser-focused on imperfections. Take a moment to soften your eyes by relaxing the muscles around your eyes and face. Allow a softer feeling to take over and notice the whole area with observation and no judgment. How does it feel?

SELF-WORTH METER

Take a moment to color in the self-worth meter based on where you see your self-love levels at this point in the workbook. Have they improved? Diminished? Write how you feel underneath the meter.

I love myself and know that I am worthy of love and belonging.

I am a work in progress and love myself most of the time.

I am learning to love myself and feel worthy but still struggle sometimes.

I feel unworthy of love and do not believe that I have anything good to offer.

How I feel about my progress so far:

_____

_____

_____

_____

WHERE I SEE MY LIFE IN ONE YEAR, FIVE YEARS, TEN YEARS

In this exercise, complete the following sections to imagine your life in the next year, five years, and ten years. Include your hopes and dreams for how you would like your life to look, and describe how you will get there.

In one year, I hope to:

_____

_____

In five years, I hope I am:

_____

_____

In ten years, I want my life to look like this:

_____

_____

Be with Nature

In this exercise, go somewhere and watch the world around you. Simply be an observer, and pay attention to the different colors, shapes, sounds, smells, and sensations you experience. Appreciate the details you might usually be too busy to notice. Notice the sounds and sights and practice being fully present as you hear the sound of a bird chirping or feel a soft and gentle breeze. Being in nature allows us to stay present in the moment and connect with the world around us. This helps us release overthinking and self-consciousness. Stop and delight in this moment.

RECIPE FOR SELF-WORTH

In the spaces provided, complete the recipe to make a special *you*. Be sure to add the finest ingredients—these should be things that make you happy and unique. If you get stuck, ask friends or family for help in reminding you of the qualities and talents that you possess.

A Sample Self-Worth Ingredient List

1 cup of authenticity
½ teaspoon of speaking my mind
1 tablespoon of humor
¾ cup of doing something musical
A pinch of creativity

Recipe Title: _____

1 cup of _____

½ teaspoon of _____

1 tablespoon of _____

¾ cup of _____

A pinch of _____

Combine the first four ingredients and mix until smooth. Add the pinch

of _____ **to taste. Bake until**

self-love and self-worth have reached desired doneness. Now share with

the rest of the world!

FIND THE GRAY AREA

Black-and-white, or all-or-nothing, thinking can make us struggle with our self-worth. We can help ourselves by finding the gray in our thoughts. To do this, let's consider using more neutral language and embracing the growing and learning parts of ourselves. It helps to find the midway point between extremes. This technique is often a more realistic, balanced, and compassionate way to think of ourselves. Fill in the squares with black-and-white thoughts, and then find your middle ground and fill in the gray.

Example: I always have to be perfect.	I always try to do my best, but sometimes I will make mistakes.	I always mess up.

WHEN DO I FEEL THE MOST LIKE MYSELF?

Think about a situation when you feel the most alive and entirely able to be yourself. What are you doing? Who is around you? What thoughts do you have? How does your body feel? Most important, how can you have more moments like these?

Describe the situation:

_____

_____

_____

_____

_____

Reflect and share how you might make more of these moments happen:

_____

_____

_____

_____

_____

DELIGHTING IN SIMPLE PLEASURES

Children have an enviable sense of wonder and amazement at the world around them. As a child, I loved chasing butterflies, spinning around until I felt dizzy, and playing rough and tumble in a little bamboo forest in my backyard. In these moments, I felt completely free to explore, using my imagination and delighting in the simple pleasures of nature. As I get older, I find myself reflecting on and appreciating these days, and have found that those early moments in my life helped me grow in my self-worth. In the box provided, draw a picture of something that you delighted in as a child. These kinds of memories can help us tap into a special place inside ourselves that thrived before the world had a chance to impact our self-perceptions.

HOBBY BUILDER

So often, our lives involve keeping up with others and hustling to the next activity. Hobbies increase our feelings of meaning and purpose and allow us time to relax and enjoy life. Following is a short list of possible hobbies and space for you to write in your own ideas. Circle each one that you've tried. Then, schedule time in your calendar to try a new hobby. Consider trying a new one every week and see what brings you the most joy.

Gardening   Yardwork   Reading   Sewing

Puzzles   Crafting   Painting

Antiquing   Cycling   Volunteering

Hiking   Coloring   Photography

Playing an instrument

Kayaking   Running

_____   _____   _____

HOW DO YOU TAKE UP SPACE?

When people feel confident and secure, they tend to allow themselves to relax and take up more space wherever they are. Pay attention to how you are sitting right now. Notice how you have your arms and legs positioned. Notice your posture, facial expressions, and eye contact. Consider the different situations listed here and describe how you might behave in them. Are you comfortable being seen? Are you able to take up the space around you? Are you comfortable in your body?

Standing in line: _____

_____

_____

Sitting in a waiting room: _____

_____

_____

Sitting at home on a sofa: _____

_____

_____

Sitting on public transportation: _____

_____

_____

Walking down the street: _____

_____

_____

A LOVE LETTER TO MY BODY

One area that is especially tricky for women involves loving our bodies as they are. Societal pressure and airbrushed and edited images of "perfection" make us feel unworthy and critical of our bodies. In this exercise, fill in the blanks with kind and positive comments about your body, to counter those negative messages in media and society.

Dear Body,

I appreciate you for exactly how you look and function at this moment. I love how

_____

_____.

I also recognize that you are powerful and strong. Thank you for always taking care of

me by _____

_____.

I especially love my arms because they _____.

Thank you to my legs for _____

and to my stomach for _____.

I know that there are times when I punish you by _____

_____.

I will try to be more loving and appreciate you every day. I love that you are mine and

I am grateful for all the amazing things that I can do with you, like _____

_____.

With love,

_____

BODY IMAGE GRATITUDE SCAN

1. Sit or lie in a comfortable position.

2. Close your eyes and take several deep breaths in and out. Allow yourself to relax as you settle into your body.

3. Starting with the top of your head, notice the sensations and feelings in this area. Send loving thoughts to your head and thank your brain for all it does to help you think and function. Reflect on your facial features and spend time appreciating each one: your mouth, nose, eyes, and ears. Thank each facial feature for what it does for you and appreciate each feature's uniqueness. If you find yourself having critical and negative thoughts, notice and observe without judgment and bring your attention back to this exercise.

4. Next, travel down your neck to your chest area. Notice this place in your body and send loving appreciation for your chest and all that it does for you. Continue with your arms, hands, and fingers. Thank them for the work they do in allowing you to move and carry things.

5. Now travel to your stomach and allow yourself to appreciate this part of your body. Say thank you for the work your stomach does in digesting your food and protecting your internal organs. Tell your stomach you are sorry if you are critical and unappreciative at times and that you are learning to appreciate your body more.

6. Next comes your bottom area. Thank your bottom side for giving you a cushion to sit on and removing waste from your body.

7. Move toward your legs and appreciate all your legs can do for you. Ending with your feet, give thanks for the hard work they do to keep you upright and moving.

8. Send a big thank you to your body, whatever its shape, size, and function. Reflect and appreciate how you are unique, and there is no one else quite like you!

EIGHT SELF-WORTH MYTHS

Correct the following statements with more helpful beliefs about self-worth on the lines below.

1. It's impossible to have self-worth and not be selfish.

   _____

2. I should love others more than myself.

   _____

3. Other people are more important than I am.

   _____

4. I must help others before I help myself.

   _____

5. Other people have influence over my self-worth.

   _____

6. The mistakes I've made define my self-worth.

   _____

7. Pleasing others is the most important thing to be worthy.

   _____

8. Self-worth comes from what others think about me.

   _____

BE YOUR OWN #1 FAN

Following are several positive statements to help you feel more confident. Read through them and choose the ones that you like the best, or that resonate most with you right now. Feel free to personalize the experience by creating your own statements in the blank spaces. Take time each day to reflect on them or post them in a visible location.

I am strong and capable.

My opinions matter, and it's okay to share them.

My feelings are valid and important.

Even when I make mistakes, I am still worthy.

I can do difficult things.

I am a problem-solver.

I deserve respect.

I am worthy of being loved by others.

I am learning to love myself every day.

It is okay for me to honor my gifts and strengths.

I am unique and special.

_____

_____

_____

_____

_____

EVALUATING BEAUTY MESSAGES

In this activity, look at different advertisements you find in magazines, in commercials, and online. Pay close attention to the images of people. Are they free from body hair, pores, wrinkles, blemishes, cellulite, etc.? Notice the size of these models and what they are wearing. Reflect on how looking at these images makes you feel about yourself. Do you want to buy the product? Did you compare yourself to the model? If you feel so empowered, try writing a letter to the magazine editor or the product's company describing your experience.

KEEP A SELF-WORTH TRACKER

Let's see how many times a week you talk to yourself in a kind, compassionate, and loving manner. In the following calendar, place a tally mark on the days that you find you are generally kind and feel positively toward yourself, even when making a mistake. Here are some examples of positive affirmations you can say to yourself every day:

I am doing the best I can.

I am proud of myself.

I did a great job.

I am getting stronger every day.

This is hard and I can do it.

I am struggling right now, but it won't be forever.

Monday	Tuesday	Wednesday	Thursday	Friday	Saturday	Sunday

LEARNING AND GROWING FROM A NEGATIVE EXPERIENCE

Sometimes it's difficult to feel worthy after we make mistakes or act incongruently with our values and disappoint ourselves. In these moments, it's so important to recognize that we are only human, and to practice self-compassion and self-forgiveness. One of the best ways to do this involves finding the lesson in the experience and recognizing where you can grow. In the following scenarios, draw a line to match each situation with the lesson or compassionate response. In the blank space, write some personal events and pair them with a compassionate self-worth lesson:

I told a harmless lie to cancel my plans.

I know this is against my values, and I am learning to make better choices. I put too much pressure on myself to be the best.

I froze when giving a presentation.

It's okay to say no without giving a reason.

No one wants to hang out with me.

It's normal to freeze when feeling scared. I can learn to relax and manage my anxiety.

I cheated on a test.

It's okay to be home alone, and I can use this time to enjoy a hobby and practice self-love.

_____

_____

_____

_____

_____

_____

_____

_____

ACCEPT YOUR FEELINGS AND MOVE THROUGH THEM

As we discussed in chapter 4, feelings are neither good nor bad. They just are. One way to develop self-worth involves increasing awareness about ourselves and our emotions. Often in suppressing our feelings, we may turn to unhealthy and maladaptive ways to numb ourselves. This response can result in unhealthy relationships and destructive coping mechanisms. In this exercise, you'll have the opportunity to identify more mindful ways to feel your feelings and move through them. Start by noticing what physical urges you tend to encounter for each emotion and then follow with how you can have a more mindful reaction..

Feeling	Urge to Act	Mindful Reaction
Example: Anger	Hit, punch, yell	Take a deep breath, relax your body, step away
Sadness		
Fear		
Joy		
Disgust		
Surprise		
Jealousy		
Frustration		

CREATE A POSITIVE SELF-WORTH CYCLE

The purple graphic shows how our negative self-talk and uncomfortable feelings can lead to maladaptive coping mechanisms or people-pleasing. In the blue cycle, fill in the blanks to create a more positive self-worth cycle.

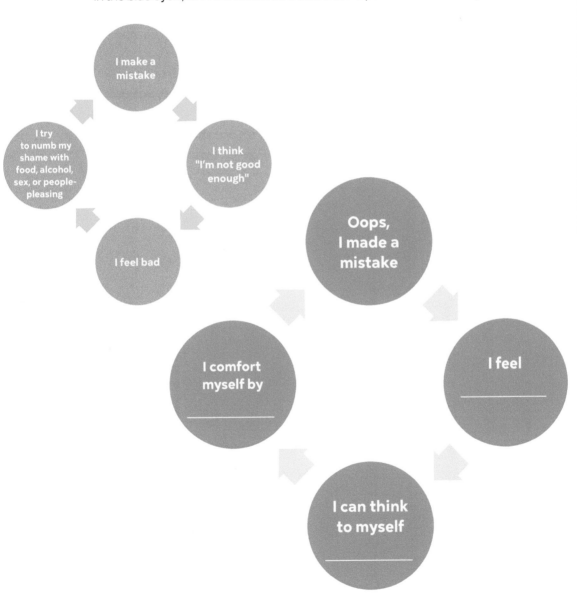

CONCLUSION

Congratulations on completing this chapter on your self-love journey. By now, you have seen how building self-worth takes effort and persistence. So often, it is easier to slide into old negative patterns and beliefs—it takes continued focus to talk in a kind and compassionate way to ourselves, as well as learn from life's challenges and the mistakes we make along the way.

Once we have a firm foundation, we'll want to examine our interactions with others. Part of self-love is creating and sustaining positive and healthy relationships. This next chapter examines what makes a healthy relationship, and discusses how to set boundaries and engage in clear, assertive communication. Buckle up—this next chapter might be life-changing.

I bring something special
to the world around me.

SEVEN

HEAL YOUR RELATIONSHIPS

"How you love yourself is how to teach others to love you."

—RUPI KAUR

As we continue deeper into the self-love journey, we'll discover an opportunity to examine our relationships and connections with ourselves and others. This chapter focuses on how to recognize the differences between healthy and unhealthy relationships, as well as identifying ways to set and maintain boundaries within our lives. As caregivers, women tend to prioritize others' feelings over their own needs. Women can also struggle with assertiveness and falling into the people-pleasing trap. By denying our feelings and needs, resentment and other toxic dynamics can emerge. A crucial component of self-love involves beginning to accept, honor, and communicate our needs and wants. When this happens, our relationships with ourselves and others can shift, opening the door to self-love, with a healthy balance of loving kindness toward others.

HOW SELF-LOVE SHOWS UP IN RELATIONSHIPS

Let's explore how having a healthy relationship with yourself can impact your relationship with others. In the space provided, consider how each of these key self-love components from earlier chapters gets reflected in relationships. Give an example of how each concept might show up in a negative way and how to make a positive change.

	Negative Concept	Positive Change
Self-worth		
Self-respect		
Self-Love		
Self-compassion		
Self-forgiveness		

UNHEALTHY RELATIONSHIPS CHECKLIST

When we are learning self-love, it's important to take time to evaluate the various aspects of our key relationships. Although we can go many years in relationships allowing the status quo to exist, when we really reflect inward and pay attention to trust, communication, and patterns of self-doubt, we can learn to identify red flags that may signal a conflict with our ability to love ourselves. By neglecting to notice or address imbalances in power and control, or a lack of mutual trust or respect, we can fall into unhealthy patterns. These red flag behaviors begin to chip away at self-esteem, potentially leading to a never-ending cycle of unhealthy dynamics. Harmful, toxic relationships breed under barren conditions where self-love fails to take root and grow. Conversely, time spent addressing these issues can serve as the springboard for a positive, even life-changing, transformation.

Check to see if any of these dynamics are present in your relationships:

❏ **Gaslighting:** Making you doubt your reality by telling you something did or did not happen or is untrue even though it is something you know.

❏ **Name-calling:** Verbal put-downs, calling you mean and hurtful names to make you feel bad about yourself.

❏ **Coercion:** Manipulating you to get their needs met without regard to your needs.

❏ **Controlling behavior:** Declaring with whom you can talk and spend time; telling you what to do, wear, feel, and/ or think.

❏ **Jealousy:** Pretending that jealous feelings mean the person loves you more, when it is, in fact, a sign of insecurity.

❏ **Threats:** Making you believe that the person will harm you in some way emotionally, socially, physically, or sexually.

❏ **Mistrust:** Showing suspicion or questioning your motives or actions.

❏ **Invisibility:** Not feeling heard or understood.

THE HEALTHY RELATIONSHIP TRIFECTA

As we learn to identify what makes up a healthy relationship, we can better understand what we deserve in our lives. In this exercise, each circle represents the crucial components of trust, reciprocity, and respect in a healthy and egalitarian relationship.

Trust, an essential element in healthy relationships, involves believing that a person is authentic, dependable, and honest. Reciprocity involves finding a balance in energy invested and received between two people. Respect involves valuing the other person with warmth and appreciation. This, of course, works best in a relationship when it's mutual, flowing both ways.

Think of a current relationship you have—perhaps with a friend, partner, lover, coworker, or family member. Consider how the elements of trust, reciprocity, and respect exist in your relationship by filling the spaces below with examples of how they show up. For example, trust is built and maintained when someone follows through on something they said they would do.

Trust

_____

_____

_____

Reciprocity

_____

_____

_____

Respect

_____

_____

_____

10 SIGNS YOU'D BENEFIT FROM BETTER BOUNDARIES

Boundaries come in different shapes, sizes, and forms. Physical barriers provide space and control over our bodies, while emotional boundaries encompass taking responsibility for our feelings. Boundary violations can occur in the context of overfunctioning, people-pleasing, and enabling. Some may think that having healthy, solid boundaries means keeping others away or not allowing others to control or manipulate us. Unhealthy boundaries work both ways. Boundary violations might also occur when we assume responsibility for another's feelings and take care of everyone else. These breaches can result in underlying resentment and anger, feelings of low self-worth, disappointment, and power imbalances in relationships. Healthy, clear, and appropriately permeable boundaries grow from self-love. The following statements reflect ways that our boundaries may be either too weak or too rigid.

Circle the number by the statements that show up in your life, and fill in the blank space with an example:

1. I get angry when others do not listen or do what I want after I keep telling them.

    _____

    _____

2. I feel responsible for making sure everyone is happy and okay.

    _____

    _____

3. I often feel resentful and angry in my relationships.

    _____

    _____

4. I shouldn't have to ask for what I need or want. Others should know.

_____

_____

5. I don't want to bother or inconvenience others.

_____

_____

6. Giving and helping others is part of what makes me unique and worthy.

_____

_____

7. I often sacrifice my wants and needs for others.

_____

_____

8. I do not let others in to know the real me.

_____

_____

9. If others knew what I was thinking, they would not like me.

_____

_____

10. I don't trust others, and close myself off quickly to relationships.

_____

_____

"SAY NO" ROLE PLAY

Do you have a hard time turning down requests? Refusing requests can feel uncomfortable, especially if we think that others might get upset. Other times, we might not believe our needs are essential. When building self-love, it is so important to learn to practice saying no. Some people feel compelled to give a reason or an excuse. Many times, though, this is not necessary. It is okay to say no and not have a reason. You don't have to justify or explain yourself. The goal is to have confidence in your decisions.

Following are some examples of ways to refuse a request without giving an excuse. In this exercise, imagine a scenario and practice standing in front of a mirror while saying one of the responses provided, or come up with your own. You can also find a real-life partner to role play with, and act out the situation to build your confidence in saying no.

Sample "No" Statements

Thanks, I won't be able to make it.

I appreciate the invitation; however, I have plans.

I can't commit to that right now.

Let me think about it and get back to you.

No, I won't be able to do that.

I am not able to at this time, but I will reconsider in the future.

I appreciate the confidence (or compliment). I am not able to.

No. That doesn't work for me.

Keep Your Boundaries Strong

The following are several affirmations that you can say aloud, keep on your phone, or post around your living space to remind you that it is okay and healthy to set boundaries. Try reading them aloud in a clear and firm tone of voice while standing up straight, with your chest out and hands on your waist like the Wonder Woman you are.

My feelings are important and relevant.

I have a right to be heard and take up space.

Others' reactions and behaviors are often a reflection of themselves and not me.

It is okay to say no without explanation.

I can set boundaries when I am overwhelmed.

I do not have to stay in an unhealthy situation.

I deserve to be treated with respect.

I can ask for what I want and need.

If someone says no or doesn't respond the way I like, it's okay.

Someone else's response does not indicate whether it was okay for me to ask for what I need or want.

I can get my needs met and still be kind.

FOUR STEPS TO ASKING FOR WHAT YOU WANT

Once we determine our worth and realize that it's okay to ask for what we want, the next step is learning how to do so. Here are four steps that might help:

1. **Focus on what you would like to happen in the encounter.** What is it that you want to accomplish? Perhaps it is to be taken seriously, request help, or ask someone to do something.

2. **Describe the situation and what you want in straightforward terms.** Depending on the relationship, it might make sense to share your emotions or explain the reason behind the request, to increase understanding.

3. **Stay focused on what you want.** At times, others will attempt to push back or refuse your request—they have the right to do this. When this happens, keep your goal in the forefront of your mind.

4. **Express appreciation for the other person's willingness to consider the request.** It doesn't matter if they comply with the request—still express thanks.

Think about a current situation with a friend, partner, or coworker. Complete the four steps that you would take in making your request in the space below.

1. Identify your goals for what you want to accomplish in the interaction. For example, I want to go to a specific restaurant for dinner.

_____

_____

_____

2. Make the request in simple and clear terms. For example, "I would like to go to an Italian restaurant for dinner, please."

_____

_____

_____

3. Stay focused on your goal. For example, the person says they just had Italian last week. "I was really hoping we could have Italian today and maybe we could try your restaurant next time?"

_____

_____

_____

4. Express appreciation for the other person's willingness to consider your request. For example, "Thank you for your willingness to get Italian food."

_____

_____

_____

Stop Apologizing

Many women overapologize and say "I'm sorry" automatically. Sometimes this happens when there are no mistakes made. Have you ever found yourself apologizing for something that you didn't do wrong? Consider the following scenario: A woman walks into the grocery store and apologizes for asking an employee where to find the mustard. In this situation, it's not necessary to apologize. Instead of apologizing for making a request, try expressing thanks. "I'm sorry, where do you keep the mustard?" turns into, "Thank you for being available. Do you know where I can find the mustard? Thank you!"

UNDERSTANDING COMMUNICATION STYLES

There are three primary communication styles. Each has a purpose and function in communication, depending on the context and situation.

Passive communication means a person does not ask for what they need, nor do they refuse unwanted requests. In cases where someone might become violent, sometimes passive communication allows us to stay safe and survive. Passive communication also can stem from a trauma response when feeling threatened.

Aggressive communication falls more along the lines of the fight response to a threat. This reaction may involve louder and stronger language and body posturing, sometimes resulting in threats, intimidation, or attacks.

Assertive communication uses calm, polite, reasonable, and firm words with relaxed and appropriate body language.

Sometimes past trauma can affect our emotions and how we communicate. Like all other animals, human brains have a fight, flight, or freeze mechanism that allows for survival. Flight and freeze responses can sometimes contribute to passive communication. Fight reactions can come out as aggressive communication. And in complex trauma situations where there is ongoing trauma, there is a fourth kind of response called fawning, which involves people-pleasing and avoidance of conflict.

In the following scenarios, circle which type of communication pattern the person uses:

1. **I don't want to bother my friend, so I don't call her for help when changing my tire.**

    Passive   Aggressive   Assertive

2. I am upset that my son did not get a spot in the school play, so I call the teacher and yell at her.

   Passive   Aggressive   Assertive

3. I honk loudly at the slow car in front of me, then cut in front of him and slam on my brakes.

   Passive   Aggressive   Assertive

4. I politely ask the waiter to make me a new hamburger that is not red inside after ordering my burger well-done.

   Passive   Aggressive   Assertive

5. I threaten to punch someone when they are taking up two parking spaces.

   Passive   Aggressive   Assertive

6. I ask my partner to please turn down the TV while I am studying.

   Passive   Aggressive   Assertive

7. I do not want to bother the waitress, so I go without a refill on my empty drink.

   Passive   Aggressive   Assertive

Answers:

1 - passive, 2 - aggressive, 3 - aggressive, 4 - assertive, 5 - aggressive, 6 - assertive, 7 - passive

WHAT IS CODEPENDENCY?

In the 1980s, Melody Beattie wrote a book called *Codependent No More*. This book allowed for a more generalized understanding of codependency and extended the definition outside of addictions. A codependent relationship happens when boundaries get so blurred over time that each person relies on the other and feels responsible for controlling another person's behavior or feelings. Rescuing, people-pleasing, "fixing," and overfunctioning behaviors and dynamics can lead to codependency. If stemming from a complex trauma history, a person learns to survive by fawning and taking responsibility for another's feelings and behaviors while denying her own. While these patterns might work for survival, over time they erode the foundation of trust, respect, and reciprocity, keys to a healthy relationship. It is possible to love someone "too much," so that you lose yourself and, in doing so, stop practicing self-love.

In the space below, write about an intimate relationship in which codependency shows up. Perhaps it is from a movie, a book, your family of origin, or your current relationship. You can even make one up if you wish. Consider sharing what each person gets from this dynamic.

_____

_____

_____

_____

_____

_____

_____

_____

PEOPLE-PLEASING

People-pleasing involves considering others' feelings, wants, and needs before our own. These dynamics have roots in feeling unworthy and hustling to be good enough.

Give examples of ways in which you people-please. You may do it without even knowing it.

At work: _____

_____

In romantic relationships: _____

_____

With friendships: _____

_____

With family of origin: _____

_____

With current family: _____

_____

In society: _____

_____

SILENCING SHAME

Often in the exploration of self-love, toxic internalized beliefs rooted in shame and feelings of unworthiness will emerge. As we've explored in earlier parts of this workbook, a variety of messages define our feelings of worth. It's important to recognize how we internalize these messages. For example, if you tell a lie, you might feel guilt, and this would help you make a better choice in the future that would align with your values. But if you lie and have a shame-based response, you would feel like a terrible person and unworthy. Shame is toxic and comes from believing we are not good enough. It means we feel unworthy of love, connection, and growth. Unlike guilt, which can propel us toward making choices that align with our values and beliefs, shame tends to push us down and paralyze us, resulting in toxic behaviors, beliefs, and relationships. As part of self-love, it's important to work to get to a point where we can say, *If I make mistakes or have faults, that means I am human!*

In this exercise, fill in the boxes to identify a time that you made a mistake and how your beliefs about yourself turned into shame.

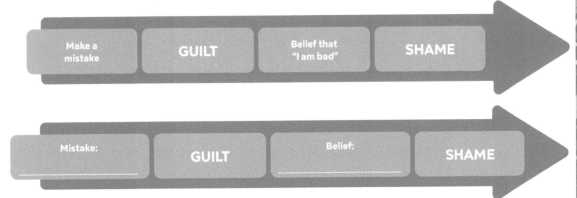

After completing this exercise, consider how you will use the information. What will you do differently as a result of your feelings of guilt? How can you think differently to help combat any shame-based beliefs? Consider previous exercises in which you practice affirmations and self-compassion. Pick your favorite self-compassion strategy and apply it to this exercise.

PURSUING UNAVAILABLE RELATIONSHIPS

Women who struggle with self-love and insecurity often find themselves in the pursuer role. This dynamic can show up in a work situation, family relationship, friendship, or with a romantic partner. The desire to feel special and have someone reassure us of our worth creates a pattern in which we chase and pursue others. This pattern may look like continually reaching out, smothering with attention, and engaging in ways to get noticed. In a work situation, it might be constantly trying to be recognized or noticed for work and needing validation of a job well done. In a family situation, it might be always making the effort to get together and accommodating everyone else's needs and preferences at the cost of your own. In a friendship or romantic relationship, it might involve always dropping what you are doing to make yourself available, or continually reaching out when the other person does not respond.

Often, the pursued pulls away, leaving us to feel even more rejection and insecurity. A dynamic develops that is rooted in what other people think about us. It becomes a trap. The more they pull away, the more we pursue; the more they pull away, the more dependent we are on them to make us feel worthy and unique.

In the space provided, describe a time in your life when you found yourself caught in this pattern.

_____

_____

_____

_____

_____

CONFLICT STYLE AND TOXIC PATTERNS

We talked earlier about passive, aggressive, and assertive communication patterns. In most situations, assertive communication allows for healthy relationships; however, there are situations when we actually need to rely on passive or aggressive reactions. Two additional toxic communication patterns can cause problems in a relationship: manipulation and passive-aggression.

When we manipulate, we are attempting to make another feel an emotion so we can get what we want. Manipulation becomes a strategy to control someone, but it uses indirect and often emotionally charged information rather than clear and direct communication. Many times, when someone manipulates, they do not state exactly what they want or need, but will play on someone's emotions. Sometimes, manipulation happens when we have tried communicating assertively and have been unable to achieve the desired results.

A passive-aggressive style of communication may emerge when we attempt to get what we want but are not transparent and open in our communication. Instead, we try to get back at someone or get revenge passively. Often this involves suppressed feelings of anger or internalized resentment. Some people resort to passive-aggressive communication when they feel powerless or that someone has authority over them. In the space provided, identify three times you have observed or participated in passive-aggressive communication and manipulation.

Passive-Aggressive:

Example: I "got back" at my partner by not doing the dishes after they complained about the house being dirty.

1. _____

2. _____

3. _____

Manipulative:

Example: Telling a friend, "I guess no one loves me," after you find out you were not invited to a party.

1. _____

2. _____

3. _____

UNPACK YOUR ATTACHMENT STYLE

Identifying the origins of how secure we feel in relationships can prove valuable in learning to have healthy interactions and connections with others. Dr. Amir Levine and Rachel Heller, in their book, *Attached: The New Science of Adult Attachment and How It Can Help You Find and Keep Love* (2010), identify the following four primary attachment styles formed in early childhood: secure, avoidant, anxious, and anxious-avoidant. These styles impact our relationships as adults and take into account our comfort levels with intimacy and closeness in relationships.

Here is a brief description of the four adult attachment styles:

Secure:

- Low on avoidance and low on anxiety

- Comfortable opening up and sharing

- Wants intimacy and connection

- Not overly worried about rejection; does not obsess about the relationship

- Does not have abandonment concerns

Avoidant:

- High levels of avoidance with low anxiety levels
- Not comfortable connecting and openly sharing with a partner
- Prefers independence and not worried if a partner becomes unavailable
- Difficulty trusting others; partner often wants them to be more intimate
- Prefers self-reliance and self-sufficiency
- Seen as aloof and disconnected

Anxious:

- Low on avoidance and high on anxiety
- Desperately craves intimacy and connection
- Often feels insecure in the relationship and desires permeable boundaries
- Fears of abandonment and rejection drive interactions; can be seen as too clingy and needy

Anxious-Avoidant:

- High levels of avoidance and high anxiety
- Worries about partner's love and commitment while at the same time being uncomfortable being too close
- Often sends mixed messages
- Wants to be close but not openly share and connect
- Worries about getting hurt if too close with a partner

Based on these descriptions, which attachment style do you think you have? Consider different relationships you have and how your attachment style plays out in the following areas:

With a romantic partner: _____

With a friend: _____

With a family member: _____

With a work colleague or supervisor: _____

With a stranger: _____

For more information, see the Resources section at the end of the book (page 153) for an in-depth test to determine your attachment style, as designed by psychologist R. Chris Fraley.

LET GO OF OLD BELIEFS

In this exercise, imagine blowing up a balloon with your relationship insecurities, self-doubts, fears, and struggles. Picture your balloon expanding as big as needed. It can even grow to the size of a hot air balloon! Once filled, imagine releasing the balloon filled with old and unhelpful beliefs. Picture this balloon floating away, and becoming smaller and smaller as it travels through the sky, until it's reduced to a tiny little speck and eventually disappears.

Fill in the balloon with some of the fears and insecurities you are most ready to let go of.

13-YEAR-OLD ME

Float back a moment to when you were 13 years old. Remember what felt important to you at the time and what consumed your energy. Recall who mattered most to you in your life and what activities you engaged in. Think about entering the lunchroom cafeteria and what you felt as you looked around for a seat.

Now imagine yourself at your current age. Do you ever feel like this young girl? Do you find yourself feeling insecure and wanting to fit in? In the space provided, share about how you have grown in self-worth since that 13-year-old version of yourself. Identify what you wish you had known then and remind yourself that as an adult, you can choose to continue to strengthen self-love.

_____

_____

_____

_____

_____

_____

_____

_____

_____

_____

CELEBRATE YOUR VALUES

As we grow and mature, our values evolve. In setting boundaries and having healthy relationships, it becomes essential to regularly check in with ourselves about our values and the things that are important to us. This clarity becomes especially crucial when we are confronted with situations that might contradict and challenge our beliefs.

In this exercise, consider what values are important to you right now. Perhaps they include trust, authenticity, or honesty, to name a few. A trick to quickly identify your values is to imagine what you would like someone to say about you if there were a huge celebration in your honor. What would you want them to say about how you treated the people in your life and how you valued your relationships?

_____

_____

_____

_____

_____

_____

_____

_____

_____

_____

_____

_____

THE OPPOSITE OF TRUST IS CONTROL

Many times in therapy sessions, I find myself saying to clients that "the opposite of trust is control." When we don't trust or believe in something, we often find ourselves trying to take control. This dynamic can have lasting impact upon relationships, as trust is an imperative component of healthy dynamics. Controlling behavior may look like micromanaging, giving advice, trying to fix and change things, or feeling responsible for others' feelings. The next time you find yourself engaging in these types of behaviors, consider what things might feel out of control in your relationship or in what ways distrust shows up. Is this something that can be handled more effectively by setting appropriate boundaries and communication, as we have learned earlier? Circle the following ways you might find yourself controlling situations in a relationship.

Micromanaging

Bossing someone around

Whining

Rescuing

Advice-giving

Fixing

Withholding feelings

Overly planning

Telling someone how they should feel

Withdrawing

Shutting down communication

A GRATITUDE NOTE TO MYSELF

As you know, it takes courage to release self-doubt and rebuild a foundation of self-worth and love. In line with practicing gratitude and self-compassion, we can thank those negative traits for trying to protect us and help us at times when we needed it, especially in our relationships. Write a thank-you letter to your self-doubt and insecurities for the ways in which they may have attempted to help you. Be sure to include in the last line that you no longer have a need for those negative beliefs anymore, and bid them farewell.

Dear Insecurities,

_____

_____

_____

_____

_____

_____

_____

_____

_____

_____

Love,

_____

CONCLUSION

This chapter may have brought up uncomfortable feelings or made you examine your relationships in a new way. Learning to love yourself sometimes changes relationships. Developing skills to set boundaries, communicate clearly, and end toxic patterns can shift relationship dynamics and patterns in ways you may not have expected. If you have discovered patterns that concern you, please reach out to get help and support. At the end of the book are resources and hotlines that can help (page 153). The most important relationship that will change, however, is the one with yourself. When you learn to say no, ask for what you need and want, and recognize unhealthy patterns, self-love is able to grow and flourish. This takes us to the final leg of our journey—the most exciting one yet, where we will combine all your hard work and honesty into a full and loving embrace of who you are.

Setting boundaries is
a way to practice self-love.

EIGHT

EMBRACE WHO YOU ARE

"I am beginning to measure myself in strength, not pounds. Sometimes in smiles."

—LAURIE HALSE ANDERSON

By now, you have hopefully experienced some thrills in learning more about yourself while appreciating beautiful insights along the way. In this final chapter, everything you have worked on will come together as you reach the last leg of the journey—fully embracing yourself. The areas covered have created a strong foundation and built skills for you to use in developing and expanding your self-love into the future. This chapter reflects on the growth you have made and clarifies all the ways you can continue to allow for the best version of yourself. We will explore your goals and dreams, and expand even further outside your comfort zone to find the space where your next journey begins.

MY UNIQUE GIFTS

An important part of fully embracing yourself involves knowing your gifts, talents, and strengths. As we have discussed, sometimes others' feedback can give us evidence to support our newfound self-appreciation. In the gift pictured here, fill in things that you love about yourself. Don't be shy. Remember, you *are* a gift!

THINGS THAT MAKE ME SMILE

An important component of embracing yourself is fully knowing yourself. While recognizing our gifts is essential, so too is knowing what makes us smile. In order to practice self-love, it helps to know what brings us happiness. Fill in the hearts with a few of those things. Consider nature, people, animals, ideas, and experiences. They could be small things, like making your favorite tea every morning or taking your dog for a walk.

LOVE YOUR QUIRKS

Part of embracing ourselves is knowing and accepting our flaws and imperfections. Imagine the power that comes from allowing ourselves to be perfectly imperfect and still know our worth. The world becomes limitless in all we can do and experience when we operate from a place of acceptance and humor, with a mindset that embraces learning and growing. Sometimes hard-learned lessons leave scars and imperfections long after the fact, and that's okay. Embracing our imperfections and quirks is an important step toward fully loving ourselves.

List five quirks or imperfections that make you special:

1. _____

_____

2. _____

_____

3. _____

_____

4. _____

_____

5. _____

_____

THINGS I AM GRATEFUL FOR ON THIS JOURNEY

Gratitude has the power to transform our perspective and improve moments of pain and suffering. Learning to find gratitude in our experiences humbles us as we grow and accept lessons along our journey. Make a list of five things that you feel grateful for as you fully embrace this self-love experience.

1. _____

2. _____

3. _____

4. _____

5. _____

EMBRACING MYSELF

Part of fully loving ourselves, as we have discussed in previous chapters, involves treating ourselves kindly and wisely. Think of ways that you do this within your established boundaries. Fill in the lines provided with examples of ways you embrace taking care of yourself.

Physically _____

Emotionally _____

Financially _____

Mentally _____

Socially _____

VISUALIZE YOUR FUTURE SELF

In the following exercise, let's visualize the older, even wiser you:

1. Close your eyes and take a deep breath by inhaling through your nose and exhaling through your mouth.

2. Think about what you long for in your life. Picture what it would take to have this dream come true.

3. Consider, in what ways are you limiting yourself? What blocks you from moving forward?

4. Imagine yourself dealing with and addressing these barriers. Visualize yourself overcoming and propelling yourself forward, closer to your dreams.

5. Imagine an older, wiser, and more evolved version of yourself reaching out to embrace you. Picture this version of yourself expressing appreciation and recognition for all you have accomplished so far. Picture your wise, older self expressing gratitude for your strength and gifts.

6. Fully embrace yourself in this present moment and know that your future self will be with you along the way.

SELF-COMPASSION TROUBLESHOOTING

When doing self-exploration activities, it's always helpful to assess and evaluate what works and doesn't work well. In these next series of exercises, we'll take some time to reflect on the core components of our self-love practice, to identify any areas that were difficult and come up with possible adjustments or improvements specific to your individual journey.

Reflect for a moment on your self-compassion practice when using this workbook. What was helpful in these exercises? What did you find challenging? Take some time to identify and list any barriers to fully embracing self-compassion. In the space after this, think about some possible solutions. This is a brainstorming session, so there are no wrong ideas. Go ahead and express yourself.

What worked for me:

_____

_____

_____

Challenges in practicing self-compassion:

_____

_____

_____

Ideas and ways to improve:

_____

_____

_____

_____

MINDFULNESS TROUBLESHOOTING

Mindfulness, a core component in the self-love journey, weaves throughout all of the exercises in this book. As you develop a strong ability to practice mindfulness, your efforts can prove life-changing by giving you the ability to live life in the moment, free from judgment and worries. What is more, mindfulness teaches us to accept and notice. To simply be. In doing so, we connect with the earth, the air, and all that exists around and within us. We become part of the bigger picture and realize how perfectly we fit within it.

What worked for me in these exercises:

_____

_____

_____

_____

I faced challenges in practicing mindfulness during this experience:

_____

_____

_____

_____

Ideas and ways to improve in practicing mindfulness in the future:

_____

_____

_____

_____

BOUNDARY-SETTING TROUBLESHOOTING

We've explored the idea that self-love does not exist without boundaries. To set limits, we must feel worthy and willing to become uncomfortable. Boundary-setting can feel scary and painful, especially when we're new to it. When boundary-setting is combined with mindfulness, we can move past this discomfort. Let's consider what worked and didn't work in setting boundaries.

What worked for me in this workbook:

_____

_____

_____

_____

Challenges in practicing setting boundaries that I have realized:

_____

_____

_____

_____

Ideas and ways to improve in setting boundaries:

_____

_____

_____

_____

FIVE WAYS TO TAKE CONTROL

As we build upon practicing self-compassion, releasing self-doubt, setting boundaries, and having healthier relationships, we can consider our options—this empowers us to take control of our lives. We have several options for how we can respond to challenges that come our way. Here are five options for how we might choose to approach and handle problems in our lives. These steps all involve acknowledging and accepting situations before we can take action.

1. **Change the situation.** Often, we can change a situation by expressing our wants and desires and communicating our preferences. While we might not always be able to alter the circumstances since we don't control others' feelings, thoughts, and actions, we know that to change something, we must take action.

2. **Tolerate the situation.** This option involves accepting and then learning to deal with things the way they are through various coping skills and perspective-taking strategies. Of course, tolerating is not synonymous with liking—it may involve circling back over time to decide if it's time for a change.

3. **Accept the situation.** In all reality, to change and to tolerate requires acceptance. However, this option of accepting the situation embraces the struggle or potential discomfort of accepting events that we cannot change. Acceptance allows for a sort of peace and requires strong mindfulness skills. It can feel empowering to accept something that can't be changed.

4. **Do nothing.** This option is simple. Do not respond to or address the situation. Ignore it completely. It's not quite the same as acceptance, since doing nothing means not working toward acceptance. For anyone who has tried to accept a situation, you know it can feel like work!

5. **Make it worse.** Hopefully, you will not choose this option frequently. Making situations worse creates short- and long-term consequences in our lives and relationships. It can create chaos and unnecessary drama.

Identify a current situation that is weighing on you. Choose one of the five life options and write about what this response might look like in your situation. Is it the best choice?

_____

_____

_____

_____

_____

_____

_____

_____

_____

_____

COMFORT ZONE

When we have the courage to reach out beyond our fears and take steps toward our goals, that is where living fully begins. Once you've embraced self-love, your life will continue to expand. The possibilities are endless. In this exercise, in the smaller inside circle, identify situations and people with whom you feel comfortable and safe. In the next circle, identify some of your limiting beliefs and insecurities. And in the third, outer circle, list all the possibilities for your growth and dreams.

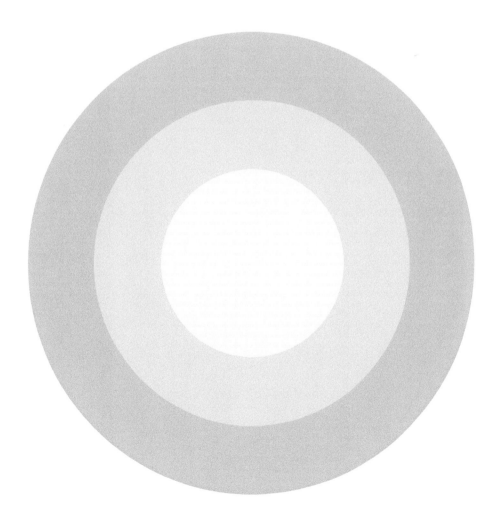

A WORK IN PROGRESS

The journey toward self-love is never-ending—we will continually grow and change throughout different developmental stages in our lives and family life cycles. This workbook can be used many times throughout your life journey, and can serve as a resource for years to come. In the space provided, identify three areas in which you feel you still need to grow, improve, and expand. Try setting a reminder in your calendar to check in with yourself every six months to see how you are doing with your self-love practice.

1. _____

2. _____

3. _____

LEARNING ABOUT MYSELF

Self-exploration can feel heavy and intense at times. When we become vulnerable and honest with ourselves, we open the door for insight and awareness to shine a light on our darkest places. Hopefully, through this workbook, you have learned so much about yourself. Take a moment and share here how you have grown personally in completing these activities:

_____

_____

_____

_____

WHO ARE YOUR HEROINES?

As we look back into history, we see countless, empowering examples of strong, courageous women who embraced self-love and change wholeheartedly. Here are some examples of women and girls, real and imagined, who represent the power of self-love. Which ones do you admire or want to be like? Feel free to list your own personal heroines. What is it about these women that inspires you?

Malala Yousafzai

Rosa Parks

Maya Angelou

Helen Keller

Annie Easley

Jo March from *Little Women*

Harriet Tubman

Anne Frank

Saint Teresa of Calcutta

Sojourner Truth

Katniss Everdeen from *The Hunger Games*

Merida from *Brave*

Wonder Woman

_____

_____

_____

_____

_____

ALPHABET SELF-LOVE SOUP

Sometimes it can be fun to play a game where you come up with words that start with a certain letter of the alphabet. In the following exercise, find positive words that begin with the letters in your name. These words should reflect what makes you unique and worthy of love. If you like, use a thesaurus or google positive words that start with each letter.

Example:

M usical

E nergetic

G enuine

A daptable

N ature-lover

MY LEGACY

Reflection is a special and vital part of your development. Reflecting on the meaning of life offers a powerful opportunity to look deep within. Sometimes reviewing our lives allows us to consider our value and purpose. This process helps find meaning with which we can align our life choices and decisions, both looking back and going forward. If you were to leave a legacy behind in the world, what difference would you like to have made? Consider ways in which you can move toward a life filled with meaning and purpose. It is here, in this space, that your self-love will shine the brightest.

My Legacy

SELF-LOVE CALENDAR

Now that you have a collection of activities for practicing self-love, try one skill a day using the calendar provided. Feel free to adapt with your own ideas, too!

Monday	Tuesday	Wednesday	Thursday	Friday	Saturday	Sunday
Write a love letter to yourself	Practice saying an affirmation	Look in the mirror and give yourself a compliment	Reach out to a long-lost friend	Practice being mindful	Listen to your Power to Women playlist	Re-read and reflect on your letters
Practice the Wonder Woman pose	Focus and repeat this mantra of the day: "I am worthy of love"	Write on your mirror that you are beautiful	Read about your favorite heroine	Think about what makes you special	Light your favorite candle and do a meditation	Name five things that you love about yourself
Try saying "No" once today	Reflect on your values and purpose	Pick a visualization activity and practice it	Take a break and rest today	Take a bubble bath or hot shower	Set a boundary with someone	Make a decision by thinking of what you want first
Ask for help once today	Move your body and appreciate it with loving thoughts	Pick a self-soothing activity and practice it	Find a more helpful thought today	Say kind words about body parts you dislike	Say something kind to yourself	Practice self-compassion by thinking how others are like you

YOU ROCK!

Complete the following letter of appreciation for your hard work, dedication, and willingness to explore self-love. This kind of work can feel uncomfortable and challenging at times. You are an amazing woman filled with many gifts and strengths, and you've taken big steps on this journey. Take a moment to express that appreciation to yourself.

Dear _____ ,
(YOUR NAME HERE)

You are truly amazing. I love that you _____

_____ .

Thank you for making self-love a priority and for taking the time to _____

_____ .

I know there were challenges along the way, like _____

_____ .

am proud of how you _____ .

You showed and learned that you have special qualities like _____

_____

and _____ .

I am impressed that you _____

_____ .

I hope you will continue growing in self-love by _____

_____ .

Thank you again for being so awesome. I love you.

Yours truly,

_____

(YOUR NAME HERE)

FIVE TAKEAWAYS INTO THE FUTURE

Write down five takeaways that you will carry with you into your life after having completed this workbook. Think about something you learned or see differently now. If you want, you can write them down on a piece of paper and pick one to focus on each day.

1. _____

_____

2. _____

_____

3. _____

_____

4. _____

_____

5. _____

_____

Quiz: How Far Have You Come on Your Self-Love Journey?

Let's take another look and see where you are now in your journey toward self-love. Rate these statements on a scale of 0 to 5 and add up the total score.

0 = never   1 = rarely   2 = sometimes   3 = frequently
4 = most often   5 = always

1. **I believe I am worthy and deserving of love.**

   0   1   2   3   4   5

2. **I believe I am special.**

   0   1   2   3   4   5

3. **I believe I have a purpose for living.**

   0   1   2   3   4   5

4. **I am able to communicate my needs and wants.**

   0   1   2   3   4   5

5. **I am accepting and loving of my body just the way it looks.**

   0   1   2   3   4   5

6. **I do not need to be in a romantic relationship to feel whole.**

   0   1   2   3   4   5

7. **I think it is okay to make mistakes and not be the best.**

0   1   2   3   4   5

8. **My feelings matter as much as everyone else's.**

0   1   2   3   4   5

9. **I place equal importance on my feelings and other people's feelings.**

0   1   2   3   4   5

10. **I deserve good things in my life.**

0   1   2   3   4   5

Scoring:

40–50 = You have achieved a wonderful sense of self-love. Keep on growing and loving yourself!

30–40 = You are on your way! Keep taking time to remember you are special and important.

20–30 = At times you feel worthy and other times you struggle. Don't give up. You are worth it!

10–20 = You struggle to feel worthy and lovable. It takes time to develop self-love. Keep going—you've got this!

0–10 = You have taken a big step toward beginning to recognize the importance of self-love. Keep practicing and growing through the lessons in this workbook. You might even consider adding extra support like psychotherapy or checking out the resources in the back of the book. Keep making self-love a priority—you deserve it!

CONCLUSION

After reading this book, I'm sure you can agree that fully embracing who we are does not happen magically. It takes time and effort to learn to let go of lingering self-doubt and insecurities and accept our uncomfortable feelings and flaws. But as we allow ourselves to learn lessons in life and practice self-love, wonderful things can emerge: a reason for living, healthier relationships, and compassion for others and ourselves. Embracing ourselves enables us to embrace others and live fully.

I am continually
growing and learning.

A FINAL WORD ON SELF-LOVE

"The most beautiful people we have known are those who have known defeat, known suffering, known struggle, known loss, and have found their way out of the depths. These persons have an appreciation, a sensitivity, and an understanding of life that fills them with compassion, gentleness, and a deep loving concern. Beautiful people do not just happen."

—ELISABETH KÜBLER-ROSS

Congratulations, you made it! While we have reached the final destination in our workbook, I hope you will continue on your self-love journey. Your courage and willingness to show up and complete these exercises and practices have undoubtedly strengthened your relationship with yourself. By now, I hope you have gained a new appreciation for your gifts and strengths. You have a better understanding of your values. Even more, you have learned ways to embrace your whole self, including your flaws and imperfections (that we all have), while releasing self-doubt. You may also have found that your relationships and interactions with others have changed. This outcome is perfectly normal and okay. With these intentional practices, you have learned new ways to continue to incorporate self-love into your daily life. It is here that your hard work pays off.

Throughout this journey, you may have encountered several roadblocks. Acknowledge your stumbles and let them go. The important thing is that you didn't give up, and you found a way to push through. Remember, this is an ongoing journey—an evolution—so just keep moving forward. Self-love has the ability to continue to profoundly change you and the world in which you live, so it's an effort worth making.

This workbook may have inspired you to look for more ways to continue to grow and evolve. I encourage you to check out the resources section at the end of this book (page 153). Many helpful books, websites, and programs are listed here to provide support and inspire you to become the best version of yourself.

I feel honored to have gotten to ride along as your copilot and help navigate your course to self-love. I am confident that you are fully ready to fly solo and set out to continue exploring your self-worth and growing in ways that enrich your life. I wish you all the best on your continued journey toward self-love.

RESOURCES

Completing a workbook like this can inspire and unlock the desire for continued growth in areas that might need more attention. Here are some resources for different topics to help you evolve on your continued self-love journey.

SELF-LOVE

Brown, Brené. *The Gifts of Imperfection.* Center City, MN: Hazelden, 2010.

——— "The Power of Vulnerability." Filmed in June 2010 in Houston, TX. TEDx video, 20:04. ted.com/talks /brene_brown_the_power_of _vulnerability.

Brené Brown is well known for her research on shame and vulnerability. Several of her books, including *Daring Greatly* and *Rising Strong*, empower individuals to find their purpose and let go of shame by embracing vulnerability. In addition to her books, Brown has several engaging TED Talks about shame, vulnerability, and self-love.

Hays, Louise. *How to Love Yourself: Cherishing the Incredible Miracle That You Are.* Read by the author. Carlsbad, CA: Hay House, Inc. Audible audio ed. 2005.

Louise Hays, a pioneer in the self-love movement, has numerous inspirational books spanning decades. She developed her own publishing company that highlights self-help books based on self-esteem.

SELF-COMPASSION

Russ Harris's The Happiness Trap website provides amazing videos and creative animations to better help people understand mindfulness and self-compassion.

His work has revolutionized the path toward acceptance and commitment to positive life changes that are congruent with our personal values. TheHappinessTrap.com

Kristen Neff, PhD, has an amazing website filled with many resources about self-compassion. It includes excellent explanations, assessment tools, and exercises to understand and practice growing in self-compassion. Self-Compassion.org

Silberstein-Tirch, Laura. *How to Be Nice to Yourself: The Everyday Guide to Self-Compassion.* San Antonio, TX: Althea Press, 2019.

SELF-AWARENESS

Personality inventories can provide a wonderful way to learn more about ourselves. Here are two websites that provide accurate assessments to help you increase self-awareness:

16Personalities.com

EnneagramTest.net

Understanding early attachment styles helps us have increased insight into our relationships. Psychologist R. Chris Fraley developed an in-depth attachment style self-assessment to help adults determine how their security and openness affect relationships:

Fraley, R. Chris, N. G. Waller, and K. G. Brennan. *Self-Scoring Adult Attachment Questionnaire.* Accessed June 15, 2020. web-research-design.net/cgi-bin/crq.pl

BODY IMAGE

Bacon, Linda, and Lucy Aphramor. *Body Respect: What Conventional Health Books Get Wrong, Leave Out, and Just Plain Fail to Understand about Weight.* Dallas: Benbella Books, 2014.

The Body Image Movement is a global endeavor to inspire people to embrace their bodies. Founder Taryn Brumfitt developed a documentary in 2012 called *Embrace* that inspires women of all shapes, sizes, and colors to love their bodies. BodyImageMovement.com

NEDA: The National Eating Disorders Association is the largest nonprofit for individuals and families struggling with an eating disorder. You will find screening tools and a helpline. NationalEatingDisorders.org

HEALTHY RELATIONSHIPS

The Duluth Model, a domestic abuse intervention program, provides wonderful resources and visual representations of healthy and unhealthy relationships called the Power and Control Wheel and the Equality Wheel. Visit their website for more information. TheDuluthModel.org

Johnson, Sue. *Hold Me Tight: Seven Conversations for a Lifetime of Love*, New York: Little, Brown and Company, 2008.

National Domestic Violence Hotline 1–800–799–7233 or TTY 1–800–787–3224. TheHotline.org

National Sexual Assault Hotline 800-656-HOPE (4673). RAINN.org

OVERCOMING CHALLENGES/ SURVIVING

Kevin Breel shares his powerful TED Talk called "Confessions of a Depressed Comic." In this inspirational message from a mental health activist, writer, and comedian, Kevin discusses his method for surviving with depression even when he seemed to have a perfect life. ted.com/talks/kevin_breel_confessions_of_a_depressed_comic.

Hamner, Ryan. *This Is Remission: A Four-Time Cancer Survivor's Memories of Treatment, Struggle, and Life*. Independently published, 2019. Ryan Hamner, a childhood lymphoma survivor, writes an engaging and personal memoir about surviving cancer. His book highlights essential ways to overcome struggles and challenges in life by staying positive and focusing on what really matters.

Roig-DeBellis, Kaitlin, and Robin Gaby Fisher. *Choosing Hope: How I Moved Forward from Life's Darkest Hour*. New York: G.P. Putnam's Sons, 2015. A powerful memoir about a heroic and inspirational first-grade teacher who saved her entire class during the tragic Sandy Hook shooting.

REFERENCES

Anderson, Laurie Halse. *Wintergirls*. New York: Viking, 2009.

Baldwin, James. *The Price of the Ticket: Collected Nonfiction*, 1948–1985. New York: St. Martin's Press, 1985.

Beattie, Melody. *Codependent No More: How to Stop Controlling Others and Start Caring for Yourself*. Center City, MN: Hazelden, 1992.

Bombeck, Erma. *Eat Less Cottage Cheese and More Ice Cream: Thoughts on Life from Erma Bombeck*. Kansas City, MO: Andrews McMeel Publishing, 2011.

Breel, Kevin. "Confessions of a Depressed Comic." Filmed in May 2013. TEDx video, 10:47. ted.com/talks/kevin_breel _confessions_of_a_depressed_comic.

Brown, Brené. *The Gifts of Imperfection*. Center City, MN: Hazelden, 2010.

Clemmer, Jim. *The Leader's Digest: Timeless Principles for Team and Organization Success*. Toronto: ECW Press, 2003.

De Angelis, Barbara. *Are You the One for Me? Knowing Who's Right and Avoiding Who's Wrong*. New York: Delacorte Press, 1992.

Hale, Mandy. *You Are Enough: Heartbreak, Healing, and Becoming Whole*. Franklin, TN: FaithWords, 2018.

Hemingway, Ernest. *Men Without Women*. 1927. Reprint, New York: Scribner, 2004.

Kübler-Ross, Elisabeth. *Death: The Final Stage of Growth*. New York: Simon & Schuster, 1975.

Levine, Amir, and Rachel Heller. *Attached: The New Science of Adult Attachment and How it Can Help You*

Find and Keep Love. New York: Penguin Putnam Trade, 2012.

Linehan, Marsha. *DBT Skills Training Manual*. 2nd ed. New York: Guilford Press, 2014.

Maraboli, Steve. *Life, the Truth, and Being Free*. Port Washington, NY: A Better Today Publishing, 2009.

Neff, Kristin. *Self-Compassion: The Proven Power of Being Kind to Yourself*. New York: William Morrow Paperbacks, 2015.

Parr, Todd. *It's Okay to Be Different*. New York: Little, Brown Books for Young Readers, 2009.

————. *It's Okay to Make Mistakes*. New York: Little, Brown Books for Young Readers, 2014.

Rogers, Fred. Middlebury College Commencement Address. May 2001. archive.org/details/rogers_speech_5_27_01

Shakespeare, William. *The New Cambridge Shakespeare: King Henry V*. Edited by Andrew Gurr. Cambridge: Cambridge University Press, 1992.

Tolle, Eckhart. *A New Earth*. New York: Penguin, 2005.

Tugaleva, Vironika. *The Art of Talking to Yourself: Self-Awareness Meets the Inner Conversation*. Soulux Press, 2017.

INDEX

ACKNOWLEDGMENTS

This workbook is a culmination of exercises and activities that I have created and used with clients throughout the years. Something truly sacred and profound happens in a therapy session while holding space for someone to share such vulnerability. It is in these moments that I feel honored, for my clients are the real teachers and healers. Extra thanks to my mom and dad, my sisters, and my children and their father, as well as those special people along the way who taught me valuable life lessons or helped encourage and inspire me to put my ideas on paper. I am genuinely and forever grateful.

ABOUT THE AUTHOR

 A native of Annapolis, Maryland, MEGAN LOGAN, MSW, LCSW graduated summa cum laude from James Madison University in Virginia with a bachelor's degree in social work and a minor in family issues. She received her master's degree in clinical social work from Florida State University. With over 20 years of counseling experience, Megan has worked in a variety of mental health settings, including domestic violence and sexual assault centers, an eating disorders program, and a local hospice program. For the past 10 years, she has enjoyed private practice, specializing in issues related to trauma and abuse, eating disorders, grief and loss, and play therapy.

A mother of two soccer-playing, teenage children, Megan enjoys spending time on the beach looking for sharks' teeth. She is a lover of boxers (the dog breed), and has a sweet cat named Jelly. In her spare time, Megan can be found attempting to play the guitar and singing slightly off-key. A daredevil by nature, she enjoys finding new adventures and spending time outdoors.

CPSIA information can be obtained
at www.ICGtesting.com
Printed in the USA
LVHW021349240221
679810LV00003B/7